TRUE
REAGAN

TRUE
REAGAN

WHAT MADE RONALD REAGAN GREAT
AND WHY IT MATTERS

JAMES ROSEBUSH

CENTER
STREET

NEW YORK BOSTON NASHVILLE

Center Street
Hachette Book Group
1290 Avenue of the Americas
New York, NY 10104
centerstreet.com
twitter.com/centerstreet

First Edition: April 2016

Center Street is a division of Hachette Book Group, Inc.
The Center Street name and logo are trademarks of Hachette Book Group, Inc.

The publisher is not responsible for websites (or their content) that are not owned by the publisher.

The Hachette Speakers Bureau provides a wide range of authors for speaking events. To find out more, go to www.HachetteSpeakersBureau.com or call (866) 376-6591.

Unless otherwise noted, all photos are courtesy of the Ronald Reagan Library. "The Prayer at Valley Forge," used at the end of the insert, is copyright of Friberg Fine Art, Inc. and is used with permission.

Library of Congress Cataloging-in-Publication Data

Names: Rosebush, James S., author.
Title: True Reagan : what made Ronald Reagan great and why it matters / James Rosebush.
Description: First edition. | New York, NY : Center Street, 2016. | Includes index.
Identifiers: LCCN 2015044801 | ISBN 9781455593828 (hardcover) | ISBN 9781478938347 (audio download) | ISBN 9781455593835 (ebook)
Subjects: LCSH: Reagan, Ronald. | Reagan, Ronald—Influence. | Presidents—United States—Biography. | United States—Politics and government—1981-1989.
Classification: LCC E877 .R68 2016 | DDC 973.927092—dc23 LC record available at http://lccn.loc.gov/2015044801

ISBNs: 978-1-4555-9382-8 (hardcover), 978-1-4555-9383-5 (ebook)

Printed in the United States of America

RRD-C

10 9 8 7 6 5 4 3 2 1

To my extraordinary wife, Nancy, and loving daughters, Claire and Lauren, who were with me on my White House adventure

CONTENTS

TRUE
REAGAN

INTRODUCTION

Where Is the Rest of Me?

He has been out of office for nearly three decades, and yet the name of Ronald Reagan is heard often today. Even as history fades and the precise details of his presidency become less distinct, many believe that the fortieth President of the United States would have answers to the complex and almost implacable issues we face today, or, at a minimum, he might have the bearing and strength of character to significantly improve global geopolitical conditions. In our extraordinarily disruptive world, Reagan is recalled as a leader who could verbally wrestle global agitators into submission. Some people look for his character traits to be represented in the voices of today's leaders. Few find them there.

In poll after poll, Reagan is referred to as a standard-bearer in leadership and communication. His public approval rating is higher now than when he left office. His overall standing has positioned him in the top ranking of those whom the public considers to be the greatest American leaders. This puts him in good company alongside George Washington, Thomas Jefferson, Abraham Lincoln, Franklin Roosevelt, and John F. Kennedy. The force of his own personality and his acts as President were impressive enough to be enduring in the hearts and minds of American citizens. And yet we sense there is more to the man that we have yet to discover. Although Reagan is referred to in the media with regularity, I have also walked down city streets and been surprised to randomly hear people of all ages talking about Reagan—usually with some curiosity, typically with respect. When I encounter strangers who learn I worked for Reagan, they typically want to tell me how much they respected him and they want to know more of what he was really like as a human being. They want to keep him alive and not have him become a mere historical statue on public display. It is almost as if they want to think of him playing a continuing role in a still-unfolding story of the America he loved so much.

The plain reality is that Reagan is not alive today to unlock the secrets of how he achieved this iconic status in leadership and communication—nor is he available to propose a platform of legislative and policy proposals to solve the various problems in which the world has become mired in the post-Reagan era. But then he never revealed his secret to achieving success in these disciplines while he was alive, either. He eschewed public introspection and confounded most anyone who attempted to decipher the source of his winning ways. Few realized that beneath that quiet demeanor was actually a brooding long-term strategist with a grand plan. He was willing to let people think what they wanted to about him. Inside he was charting a course for himself and the world based on beliefs he established in his early life. He did not strive for personal popularity. *He wanted American values to be popular.* He attached himself to these values as if he were holding on to the horn of a saddle as he rode the uptick in public popularity because of his political horsemanship. It was a brilliant strategy that American leaders since Reagan have almost completely missed. It was his own genius. The Reagan way. Not found in any textbook, on any website, or in political training, and yet simple, direct, and accessible.

People have asked me: What would Reagan do if he were alive today—about one of the many fearsome trouble spots in the world? How would he handle these conflicts? What answers would he have? What kind of Oval Office speech could he give to make us feel better about the situation? How would he manage U.S. bilateral and multilateral relationships? How would he take control and exercise the strength required to deter aggression against the U.S. and our allies? How would he unite us rather than divide us?

The only reasonable answer to this type of speculation is to look back at his record, practice, and principles. From these we could discern that since Reagan proved himself a brilliant strategist—though he was not heralded as one while in office—a fierce competitor on the verbal battlefield, effective in developing and maintaining useful personal relationships with other leaders, and an eager delegator of responsibility, he would have a powerful response to contemporary challenges. I believe Reagan would have offered a muscular deterrence to leaders who would encroach on the universal values he held to be most important and championed—individual freedom from oppressive and overreaching government control, and personal liberty. Whatever political leader and whatever system got in the way of these God-given rights, as Reagan saw them and referred to them, he targeted as the enemy or evil.

Yes, he protected Americans, but what's more, his efforts were designed to help individuals suffering under totalitarian regimes anywhere in the world. The facts bear this out.

Reagan's political beneficiaries are found in many parts of the world. Reagan loved America and believed in its exceptionalism, but he also wanted everyone in the world to enjoy what Americans do. He wanted the light from the "shining city on a hill" he believed America represented to be shed around the globe. He knew that safeguarding and spreading democracy outside of the United States was the best way to protect Americans and the freedoms we enjoy. He never retrenched. He never yielded authority to anyone who did not operate in the best interest of the American people and American values. He loved his country and his countrymen too much not to keep them safe.

Since the time Reagan occupied the Oval Office, no one in American politics has been able to equal his oratorical ability and assume the mantle of *The Great Communicator*, as he was dubbed by the media. But earning this honor was due to more than being a mere thespian, effectively mouthing the sometimes grand and picturesque thoughts of others. Reagan wrote hundreds of his own speeches in longhand on yellow legal pads (which survive to this day), researched their content, and spoke from his heart and mind—long before there were any professional speechwriters on board. In actuality Reagan was the Great Communicator far before he moved into the "home above the store"—as he and other Presidents have called the White House. Starting in the early 1950s, Reagan was publicly explaining his vision for America everywhere he was invited and some places where he was not—most notably in Hollywood. His beliefs were not political contrivances suddenly concocted for his presidential campaigns. They were observable in his communications before he even dreamed of a run for the presidency.

People tend to think of Reagan as having had one career prior to reaching the White House—that of movie actor—and while that job experience proved useful in his ultimate and final position, it was in a much earlier homegrown role, growing up as the son of a preacher in small Midwestern towns, that gave Reagan his basic and most durable communication skills—as well as his personal principles. He learned early to copy and adopt the oratorical skills of his mother, who was a substitute minister and small-town actor, and to a limited extent he also mimicked his father, who was quick with Irish humor as well as a ready and picturesque storyteller himself. Reagan developed his capabilities and ideals for leading and communicating at home growing up; over his lifetime, he expanded and refined them in his jobs as lifeguard, radio sportscaster, film actor, union organizer and leader, corporate spokesman, Las Vegas nightclub performer, and two-term governor.

What I have written is based on what I saw and heard during my days working for the Reagans. I am also sharing what the President revealed to me personally, face-to-face. These one-on-one encounters shaped and informed my view of how he came by these strongly held beliefs or standards, as well as the uncommon courage to employ them boldly for the benefit of society. Until Reagan occupied the White House, the world had not seen these exact qualities in a twentieth-century statesman since Winston Churchill, nor have we seen them since. Like Churchill, Reagan's story is all about his values and character: how he developed and tested them; how he suffered to establish them; and finally how he created, affected, and delivered governmental policy based on them—and thereby changed history.

Great leadership and communication carry and deliver

a message and moral energy. The ability to achieve positive change is fundamentally dependent upon the values and character of the leader. Leaders are ultimately remembered by the effects or results of their work and the examples they leave behind. Often they are more completely understood after they leave office. That was what happened to Winston Churchill who, despite having led England to victory in World War II, was shockingly turned out of political office at the end of the war, but is now universally lionized for his outsized accomplishments, his soaring and inspiring oratory, and his character.

But Churchill, a more colorful character who was in public service far longer, defined himself much better than Reagan through his prolific published writings, his thousands of public speeches that included personal reflections and professions of his own fears and vulnerability, and his leadership of the British to victory in World War II. Though born in a palace, Churchill lived a life of public service and was often accessible to the average man—especially during the war. As a result he has been comparatively easier for biographers to write about and the public to understand than Reagan—although even in Churchill himself there also remains a degree of mystery.

Reagan, with a much simpler résumé than Churchill, made himself more difficult to understand because he was not publicly introspective, was relatively colorless, largely scandal free, left few genuinely interpretative writings or interviews, and did not lead a nation into or through a great war. Yet even though much of his private personality remains unmined, his public standing continues to climb. The fact is that although few really understand Reagan from the inside out, he has become a standard against which other leaders are now compared—that is, he set a standard, in some categories, of an ideal American President.

This book uncovers and defines some of these unique and vital, yet hidden, Reagan characteristics and draws a link between his leadership record and the human, moral, and spiritual values and belief systems on which he built a successful political career. In order to comprehend the standards and precepts by which he lived, led, and communicated, we need to begin by discovering more about the internal workings of the man. This helps frame and illuminate the unique background that formed Reagan's principles by which he lived and set his own unique creed as a leader. His life and his values are inseparable from what he was able to accomplish in public office, and that is the greatest Reagan leadership lesson of all. Reagan's beliefs provide a road map to his genuine core. Even though he had been a celebrity and in the media for decades, he could never completely escape the features of his upbringing, which extolled virtue and suppressed personality. In a way, he never left the Rock River in Dixon, Illinois, where he spent seven summers as a teenage lifeguard. During that time he saved seventy-seven swimmers threatened by rip currents and sometimes choppy waters. I believe he always saw himself as a lifeguard—ultimately on a much larger river—on a larger mission. Reagan the Lifeguard. It explains a lot.

Another apt and figurative role that fits Reagan was that of standard-bearer. Standard-bearers have, throughout history, literally and mythically led the charge into battle, always carrying the standard or flag of the advancing army. As a type of standard-bearer, Reagan was a warrior for his beliefs. He carried a proclamation of what he understood to be the best American values. He was courageous in his willingness to go to battle over ideals—when he thought it was warranted—for the cause of freedom and democracy in the world. Reagan carried that flag with clarity of purpose, with pride, and with love for the country he represented. He also almost sacrificed his life for this country as an assassin's target.

This is a book about the future as well as the past. There have been seismic shifts in American culture and global politics since Reagan lived at 1600 Pennsylvania Avenue, but the moral, spiritual, and intellectual precepts of great leadership should not be locked up like quaint features of the past. They are elements required of every time and of any free society. This book is not so much a visit to the past as it is an examination of the components of leadership needed for the future—all based on Reagan's character and record.

People have their own views about what made Ronald Reagan great—or not great. However, my hope is that what I have written will at least stir a discussion about the essential components of great leadership and how they can become a more prominent part of our current and future global community. What actually made Reagan great—and he would have been hardly as great otherwise—was his character, which was furnished and nourished by his inner convictions, standards, and beliefs. Reagan's life and leadership provided a useful example of the depth of thought and personal commitment, deployed in an impersonal and humble way, that are needed in local communities as well as on the world stage.

Reagan was called aloof, friendless, cold, and uncompassionate by his opponents, in just the way that Abraham Lincoln was caricatured. Reagan was also portrayed as intellectually inferior because of his prior profession, just as Lincoln was for his lack of formal education. Reagan was even derided by conservatives as not being conservative enough. Some of these labels were political fabrications. Some merit consideration. In this book, a discussion of his inner character will address some of the lingering doubts and questions about his leadership ability. This book will expose where his gift for leadership came from, how he prepared for it, how hard he actually worked at it, how competitive he was, and ultimately why he is attaining a higher stature in world opinion where many of the traditional features of leadership he bore are rapidly disappearing.

CHAPTER ONE

His Beliefs Were His Arsenal, and Words His Weapons

On September 1, 1983, two years into his first term as President, while Reagan was vacationing at his beloved Santa Barbara, California, ranch, the Soviet Union decided to awaken a drowsy world with its terrorist downing of Korean Air Lines Flight 007. The Boeing 747 was a passenger jet flying from New York to Seoul, South Korea, carrying one member of the United States Congress and 268 other passengers and crew members from various countries. After stopping in Anchorage, Alaska, for refueling and after a change of routing, the plane mistakenly veered into Soviet airspace and, after a short volley of radio communication, was shot down by a Russian fighter pilot over the Sea of Japan. This jarring and deliberate act on the part of the Soviets came on the heels of Reagan's now iconic, but fiercely controversial at the time, "Evil Empire" speech. That speech had been delivered a few months before in Orlando, Florida, on March 8, and it was the perfect oration to presage and frame this incident. The Soviets had now handed irrefutable evidence to Reagan and the rest of the world that they were in fact an evil empire. This incident helped to verify the charge in Reagan's speech.

Mike Deaver, his longtime closest aide and friend, related to me afterward that he pressed an unhappy Reagan into an early retreat from his wood splitting and brush gathering at his small adobe-style ranch house high in the picturesque Santa Ynez Mountains, back to the grave and serious dark-paneled and windowless White House Situation Room—located in a bunker in the West Wing basement. Once there Reagan, in surprising opposition to the impatience of his advisors, was not quick to approve any orders for immediate and specific retaliatory action. Reagan typically took the long view of history while making short-term policy decisions. He frustrated the assembled officials—who were urging decisive and immediate action by the American leader—by suggesting a better course was to wait and assess how the rest of the world recorded and responded to this violent act and to then determine the retribution, if any, from other quarters before he took any bold action himself. The trigger-happy hawk, as he was regarded by some, took his own turn onto a course of using other countries and multilateral voices around the world to convey his own shock and alarm—but not for long.

He was strategic in taking this measure of global response, because he saw this deliberate act of terror as an opening to not just condemn this specific action but to link it to the broader evil of communism. He used his political capital to take another whack at what he had characterized as an evil system and make a worldwide schoolroom lesson from it. He preferred to look at this incident in the context of his long-term plan to defeat communism—or, better said, let it defeat itself, with some help from him, his government, and a small group of other world and religious leaders.

But the world did not have to wait long to hear from him about this incident, nor did he parse his words when he spoke directly to the nation for sixteen dramatic minutes from the Oval Office. In his remarks he drew a vivid picture of the recklessness and immorality of this shocking act. Reagan had felt that way about what the Soviets did from the moment his national security advisor reported it to him. He waited, though, for the right moment to respond, when other leaders were mostly done speaking, to launch his verbal salvo of disgust. There was no disguising how he felt when he went before the cameras, in the Oval Office, to sum up what he thought.

He appeared sober and concerned. This was not a watered-down, rambling statement. His words were like heat-seeking, confrontational missiles. His words, but more his beliefs, locked onto and hit the target. The verbal strikes were specific and unequivocal. He included a substantial list of actions he was taking and actions he was asking the United Nations and allies the world over to initiate as a result of the downing of KAL 007. His presentation to the American people on September 5 reflected his view that standards of human behavior had been broken, standards that he supported unwaveringly. He also cleverly played the tape of the pilots in the Soviet attack plane, which showed they had clearly executed a deliberate act while describing it in detail to an alarmed ground crew.

It was critical that Reagan played that tape in the wake of continual Soviet denial of their complicity in the tragic downing. Again, he was attempting to let an evil system destroy itself by dramatically unmasking and exposing it in plain sight to the world. He was betting on widespread moral repudiation from a moral audience. He let the Soviet downing be prosecuted in the court of global public opinion. Importantly, Reagan believed in empowering his constituency through his oratory, because he respected them. He was a uniter. He attempted in every talk to bring Americans together to project a position of strength to the world. He knew he needed more than the power of his words to win his way in the theatre of global opinion. He needed the American people behind him and with him.

To place this incident in a global context, which was typical of his strategy with most issues, Reagan said that night from the Oval Office in the following excerpts I have reordered to emphasize their importance:

"And make no mistake about it, this attack was not just against ourselves... This was the Soviet Union against the world and the moral precepts which guide human relations among people everywhere. It was an act of barbarism, born of a society which wantonly disregards individual rights and the value of human life and seeks constantly to expand and dominate other nations...

"Let me state as plainly as I can: There was absolutely no justification, either legal or moral, for what the Soviets did...

"But despite the savagery of their crime, the universal reaction against it, and the evidence of their complicity, the Soviets still refuse to tell the truth... Indeed, they've not even told their own people that a plane was shot down."

During his remarks he referred to the U.S. Congress with respect as *"that distinguished body"* and continued his bipartisan reach by quoting from former Democratic Senator Henry "Scoop" Jackson (D-WA) and also from President John F. Kennedy. Finally, seeking to draw the listeners up close and to unite them, he ended this way:

"Let us have faith, in Abraham Lincoln's words, 'that right makes might, and in that faith let us to the end dare to do our duty as we understand it.' If we do, if we stand together and move forward with courage, then history will record that some good did come from this monstrous wrong that we will carry with us and remember for the rest of our lives."

Who was this President who had the uncommon ability to stake a position so boldly and with such conviction? Few people understood the man captured by the camera lens sitting behind his massive oak desk, but they could agree he did have the ability to engage an audience with his message.

Reagan has remained in death as he was in life: a uniquely compelling and extraordinarily gifted world leader on the outside, but with an enigmatic interior. His life—that is, his personality—was unsettling and incomprehensible to some biographers. His mostly quiet inner character seemed out of bounds for them. For most people, including even some who worked for him and had known him for years, he was just plain hard to figure out. It wasn't that he was unusually complicated; it was that he was usually uncomplicated. The trouble arose from the fact that he never really talked about himself, especially in ways that might have revealed what he was thinking. He did not lead a personally interpretative life—at least as much as we know from hints about what he was thinking and the things he shared with me individually, in official meetings, and in what he said to his wife in my presence. He kept a mental distance, cordoned off from and frustrating his long-suffering official biographer, Edmund Morris, who threw up his hands in exasperation over a subject he described to journalist Lesley Stahl as "one of the strangest men who's ever lived. Nobody around him understood him. I, every person I interviewed, almost without exception, eventually would say, 'You know,

I could never really figure him out.'" This was despite Morris's having conducted thousands of hours of interviews and research that resulted in an equally strange eight-hundred-page book on the fortieth President.

My experience with Reagan and my interpretation of his character was decidedly different from that of Morris and some other well-meaning and scholarly writers. Because I had the responsibility for starting the domestic policy program most reflective of Reagan's personal values, he took an extraordinary amount of time to explain to me what those values were. Because I also traveled the world with the President and First Lady, had an opportunity to engage them at certain reflective points, and to ask him, especially, about his personal and sometimes unofficial views on various topics, his guarded and complicated persona seemed more plainly accessible to me.

Reagan rarely reflected publicly upon or discussed what was going on inside his discreet mind, and even today he is known not so much for who he was but rather by what he accomplished. *And that was just the way he wanted it.* The reason, however, that it is crucial to define the interior of the man is that this is where his principles originated—from carefully adopted precepts, learned and acquired in early boyhood, adolescence, and college, then refined, tested, revised, and put to work over a lifetime. These principles informed and shaped the decisions he made as an American and a global leader that affected millions of people. To complete the picture of Reagan as a leader, we need to knit these two sides of the man together.

While some heads of state are measured solely by their actions, politics, or intellect, it was Reagan's personal character and particular belief systems that account for his success as President. He would have been a failure at political leadership without them. And yet, even with these character elements so critical to his success, little is still known about these rock-solid pillars of his thinking, to which he was so irresistibly committed. This inside look—defining Reagan by his principles, and defining his principles by understanding his inner character—is the type of Reagan assessment that has been largely missed, even by many who knew him and worked with him. Reagan himself was of little help to others who could have defined him. Even Mike Deaver, who knew him for thirty-five years, titled his book about Reagan *A Different Drummer.*

I will never forget the initial unveiling of the official White House portrait of the President—a large oil painting. Sadly it had to be sent back to the artist, rejected because of its obvious unlikeness to the real Reagan. In fact the Reagan Library has a gallery of Reagan portraiture that attempted but often did not capture the accurate likeness of the President. Good portrait painting usually conveys something of the character of the subject in addition to an accurate or representational physical resemblance. Many artists have had a difficult time painting Reagan with success. He is as challenging to depict in physical reality as in metaphysical topography.

Now, for the first time, there is an entire generation for whom Reagan is only an archetypal historical figure or an icon. For them he is not recognizable through direct experience. Since the private Reagan was left largely unnarrated by him throughout his life and he was almost totally silent about it during his presidency, it is more difficult to grasp what he was really like. However, this quiet disposition provides indispensable clues to the interior principles he lived by and that directly affected his exterior actions. This is why I am so frequently asked: "What was Reagan really like?"

Like most public servants, Reagan left a trail of documented official evidence—records that detail his actions as
well as those that speak to his character; however, he did not
fit the puzzle pieces of his character together, nor did he reveal,
directly or interpretively, much about his private identity or his
rationale for making decisions. He never painted a particularly
discerning literary self-portrait, although he did write auto-
biographically about the facts of his life—out of necessity, in
campaign-styled volumes. He left it for us to attempt to create
a more complete picture of the personal qualities that defined
his character—and these features, assembled together with his
official record, result in a total picture of the man. Few leaders are ever one-dimensional—Reagan included. However,
what some historical figures accomplished in public life and
left in the public record satisfies an appetite for biographical
portraiture.

All leaders make decisions based on subjective views, opinions, values, education, personal experiences, and beliefs.
Reagan was no exception. These beliefs directly formed, supported, and gave energy to his acts as President. For Reagan,
though, his faith in and everyday dependence on a Higher
Power and his love of America were so merged and woven into
his leadership and communication style that he could be better
characterized as a political missionary, the son of a preacher,
than a political head of government.

Reagan saw himself as an evangelist for the precepts and
moral teachings in which he believed and by which he lived;
however, he mostly communicated his beliefs by quoting the
words of others—words that he carefully and deliberately
deployed in strategic ways for a political purpose. He would
frequently repeat quotations from historic thinkers, patriots,

or writers to make certain his audience understood the import of his message. Using this technique—liberally quoting from grand, reliable, and universally accepted and renowned figures—resulted in more of a message delivered *through* him than actually *by* him. It was, however, decidedly effective, and it added power and import to his speeches—to depend on other thinkers who might enjoy the broad support that history sometimes bestows. In this way he was also utilizing a trusted acting technique to become a reliable and believable character who employs the words of the screenwriter—never or rarely his own. However, in the case of Reagan as President, he was using the words of others that happened to reflect his *own views*. But Reagan could never have been successful in selling his potent brand of politics if he had been just speaking words others thought or wrote for him. For him the words he spoke were direct extensions of his own beliefs.

This unique Reagan communications tool is observable in almost every speech and statement he gave while in office. In this example, in commemoration of Captive Nations Week in 1983, he said:

"Twenty-five years ago, the United Nations Declaration of Human Rights proclaimed that 'all human beings are born free and equal in dignity and rights.' This reaffirmed an eternal truth that Thomas Jefferson in 1776 wrote into our own Declaration of Independence. Another great thinker, Edmund Burke, observed simply that 'the cause of Freedom is the cause of God.' Some twenty-five centuries before, the prophet Isaiah admonished the world 'to bind up the broken-hearted, to proclaim liberty to the captives.'"

And again in announcing his own Bill of Economic Rights in 1987, Reagan said:

"Jefferson, in his first Inaugural, spoke for his countrymen when

he said, 'A wise and frugal government, which shall restrain men from injuring one another, which shall leave them otherwise free to regulate their own pursuits of industry and improvement, shall not take from the mouth of labor the bread it has earned. This,' he said, 'is the sum of good government.' Well, that vision of America still guides our thinking, still represents our ideals."

Reagan lavishly used these quotations from others to reinforce a point of view, for dramatic effect, and in order to gain enough gravity to enable him to take the actions he thought were correct while in office. He used some of these famous quotations for political cover—shining by the borrowed light of those already mostly universally acclaimed.

I often hear people say, almost with a resigning sigh, "We always knew where Reagan stood on an issue and we liked that whether we agreed with him or not. He was not a moving target." Generally people see and respond well to stability and strength. They felt that way about Reagan because he usually explained where he stood on an issue—in plain terms over and over again, deliberate repetition being the mark of an effective communicator. Reagan never vacillated and rarely reversed his views on broad basic principles. Typically he carefully explained his detailed rationale for taking action, almost to the point of boring his audience, in an effort to educate the listener and to build a base of support. This practice is in stark contrast to a majority of leaders who do not adequately explain their actions or rationale, perhaps because they don't really understand them themselves.

In an article published in a journal called the *Strategist*, professional communications consultant C. Peter Giuliano called Reagan "a master of clear, concise, credible communication." He went on to say that "Reagan was always certain about his purpose. He maintained a sure vision of America and what he wanted to accomplish. He kept his messages short and clear. His speeches were not laden with more facts and data than people could quickly absorb. If he had been a corporate CEO, his vision of what he wanted his company to achieve and how he wanted it to behave would have been clear."

Even Reagan's immediate predecessor, President Jimmy Carter, not especially long-suffering in defeat after just one term in the White House, said of Reagan, "[He] provided an inspirational voice to America when our people were searching for a clear message of hope and confidence... He had unshakable beliefs and was able to express them effectively, both in America and abroad."

While everyday men and women also praised Reagan for his communication skills, professional elocutionists, trainers of public speakers, and even his political opponents also hailed the fortieth President's ability to talk. My friend Merrie Spaeth, a former film actress who once worked for Bill Paley, the legendary President of CBS, and who is now, herself, a highly sought-after professional communication and message trainer in Dallas, Texas, told me that Reagan "got it all right without appearing to try. He never labored over his words but spoke from conviction. He was measured but never unsure. His voice had a moderate, comfortable tone, not forced, that drew the listener in. This stood out from the typical politician who tends to speechify by yelling, possibly mimicking the worst type of circuit preacher or televangelist. His phrasing was pitch-perfect and you got the message on the first try, from listening to him. I use him as a role model every day in training business people and others."

The fortieth President of the United States set a high standard with his extraordinary ability to talk and be heard. He moved and motivated people through his communication and mainly because of his strongly held and heartfelt beliefs and his ability to deliver them verbally and nonverbally. Since his days in public office ended, other political leaders and public speakers have often sought to emulate Reagan's ability to inspire; however, most of them have failed. For aspirants to public service in either political party, Reagan has been a role model. Republicans, especially, want to stick close to him because he was a gigantic winner of political campaigns. Labels are often applied to Presidents, become embedded in history, and are perpetuated through generations as a short-hand reference tool. George Washington was "Father of a Nation." Abraham Lincoln was a "Liberator." FDR was a "New Dealer." Eisenhower was a "Soldier President." Reagan, whose first label was "Actor President," assumed "Great Communicator" and "Teflon President" as his labels during and after his two terms in the Oval Office.

The Great Communicator label was even more often used in reference to him in retirement. It was then that more of his own personal writings, including private letters and hundreds of handwritten speech drafts, were discovered—almost accidentally—by researchers at Stanford University. These documents have provided evidence that Reagan wrote hundreds of his own speeches and carefully constructed, tested, and validated his beliefs in words and public presentations. The ideas were his own. The writing was his own. Even his personal love letters to his wife, Nancy, were published—revealing how the man felt and communicated within his marriage. This was far from the characterization of Reagan as personally unsympathetic and without feeling—a person who was merely mouthing the extraordinary words of brilliant speechwriters.

His own speechwriting and delivery began in a structured and formal way before and during his long tenure as a Screen Actors Guild board member and then as its President. It continued through his years as public spokesman for General Electric (GE)—on what was called the "mashed potato" dinner circuit and at the GE factory gate—as well as later in his two terms as governor of California and finally as the American President. He had a prominent hand in crafting and forming his speeches as well as editing them—as so many speech drafts with his handwritten notes substantiate.

A Vantage Point from Which to Learn about His Character

When I joined the Reagan Administration and the President's staff in 1981, I knew almost nothing about the President and First Lady. I had read about them and watched them on television, but that was of little help when it came to working directly for them every day. I voted for Reagan—of course—and my wife and I were guests of the Reagan campaign at one of the formal 1980 presidential debates held in Cleveland, where we were living at the time. I had also not been introduced to the Reagans personally, or for that matter any of the Californians from their days in Sacramento and Los Angeles, who were much more knowledgeable about them and savvy about their habits and personalities.

While that lack of experience put me at a disadvantage in many ways, it also gave me an added measure of curiosity about my new clients and provided me with a dogged determination to figure them out—if for no other reason than to keep my job and to be more effective in working for them in the White House. I started my Reagan education by listening carefully to the First Couple and watching intently—and in time they revealed themselves to me, sometimes unintentionally and sometimes through focused probing on my part. Ultimately I was left to my own devices to piece together a better picture of who they were and where they were coming from in the decisions they made and how they lived. I did this initially from my post managing the President's favorite domestic policy program.

The Private Sector Initiatives (PSI) program, the government program on the domestic side closest to Reagan's heart, had been a part of his 1980 political platform and was also included in the Heritage Foundation's massive thousand-page playbook, *Mandate for Leadership: Policy Management in a Conservative Administration*. I also learned later that Reagan had, through the years prior to coming to Washington, referred informally to the phrase *private sector initiatives* in speeches now available in the Ronald Reagan Presidential Library. This was his own term for the fact that the private sector often provided better solutions for social problems than the government could by itself. Finally, after being elected President, Reagan had an opportunity to convert this idea into an actual program—which I had the privilege of launching and managing for him.

Once situated in my White House office, I wrote a comprehensive plan and Presidential Decision Memo for the formal adoption of PSI. It was to include a small staff and a blue-ribbon Presidential Commission. We presented the plan to the President one weekend at Camp David; he wholeheartedly endorsed it and pledged his personal and direct everyday engagement. To underscore the importance of this program to the President, Jim Baker, Mike Deaver, and Ed Meese—the three most powerful men in the White House at the time—traveled with me on Marine One, the President's helicopter, up to the fabled Catoctin Mountain retreat to make the pitch to the President over lunch. To be clear, there were many more critically important initiatives being managed out of the West Wing and throughout Cabinet agencies, and with far greater urgency—and yet this tiny program, by comparison to the others, bore the stamp of Reagan's personal character.

The goal of PSI was to stimulate the private sector, including business and philanthropic leaders, to find new and innovative ways to address public needs such as education, housing, and healthcare more effectively than had been done by the government acting alone. This was a genuine Reagan priority, and he saw it as a key element in his domestic policy program. Coincidentally, and happily for me, it was also the focus of my career in philanthropy and business prior to joining the Administration. It was this program that helped to usher the term *public-private partnerships* into play more prominently in public policy, and through an executive order we were able to direct a small percentage of each Cabinet agency's discretionary budget to fostering these partnerships as a better way to spend public tax dollars and secure a better return on the investment of public funds.

My involvement with this program, so aligned with Reagan's personal and yet little-understood character, is what began to open a window for me on, and piqued my curiosity about, Reagan's belief system. How Reagan felt about PSI and what he discussed with me about this initiative helped solve for me some of the mystery about his character. It also added transparency to his controlled and inwardly quiet but out-wardly talkative personality.

During the second year of Reagan's first term, I was asked by Mike Deaver to also assume an additional role of Chief of Staff to the First Lady. This was the first time in White House history that a Chief of Staff on the First Lady's team would also hold a senior post with the President. This worked well, because it helped to create a good working relationship between the West Wing and the East Wing, and it smoothed out what I learned had been troubled waters in earlier presidential admin-istrations between the two staffs. It also worked especially well for this particular President and First Lady team, because of her keen interest in his schedule and official activities, and because the President's other advisors often wanted to solicit and hear her opinion on various issues. In this expanded role, I was a part of the President's senior staff and a Deputy Assistant, serving on the long-range scheduling team, the Theme for the Day team, and the preadvance negotiating teams for foreign state visits; I was also a part of the early-morning senior staff meetings and briefings convened by the President's Chief of Staff. These duties included managing the official life of the First Lady, managing the East Wing staff, and traveling and working with both of the Reagans.

Among the things I learned about the First Couple and how they worked was that when they were a part of the film indus-try studio system, they had a staff to direct them, dress them, light them, photograph them, provide them with cue cards, scripts, and talking points, publicize them, and advance them. The studio system often provided an array of these types of people and services to support actors when they were working on a film—and this was at no financial cost to the actors personally; it was just the way films were made. That translated later into a White House staff that performed in similar roles.

Ultimately I learned more about the similarities between Hollywood and Washington, DC, where the major players are politicians, not actors, and where there are entire industries to support them—just as ubiquitous as those who worked on the back lots and in the production studios of the film industry. Once I figured this out about Hollywood, Washington, and the Reagans, it was easier for me to feel comfortable with and accept the way they thought and worked.

Their experience in the film industry also gave them a big advantage in knowing how to *run* the American presidency—something Reagan's immediate predecessor lacked, which was a particular appreciation for the tools of *staging* the presidency. Later Bill Clinton himself followed the Reagan playbook for how to *be* an American President—almost to a T. He employed Reagan's communication strategy effectively, and through his daily introduction of new programs and policy initiatives he dominated the news as Reagan had through his Theme for the Day strategy.

Clinton's self-professed role model was John F. Kennedy, and the Kennedys also had an ability to stage the presidency. This was one reason there were some similarities noted between the Kennedys and the Reagans. A mutual feeling of respect and interest was often shared between them, as I saw firsthand at several events and in other communications between them, some of which came through my office.

I saw evidence of this relationship several times, such as during the twenty-fifth anniversary commemoration of the Special Olympics Program, which the Reagans hosted for the Kennedy family on the South Lawn of the White House in

1983. I saw this friendship again during the President's visit to the Kennedy home in McLean, Virginia, for a John F. Kennedy Presidential Library fund-raiser. There was an easy affability and understanding that came perhaps from some of the Hollywood influence both families had shared, and also from a sense that both Administrations were about new platforms and ideas as well as a perception of the strength and exuberance of the American presidency that was a part of both families.

With an understanding and appreciation of the power of words and the images that accompany them, Reagan, like Kennedy and later Clinton, deployed them effectively and for targeted political purposes. President Lincoln himself, although he did not have television to convey his ideas and gave only one hundred speeches during his tenure, wanted—according to the Morgan Library in New York, which hosted a 2015 sesquicentennial appreciation of him—"words that appealed to reason, not mere emotion...[and] writing that was clear and cogent, and that, when spoken, was pleasing to the ear... Lincoln saw the power of rhythmic repetition...[and] had no appetite for grandiloquence and pretension." With his two powerful speeches, the one at Gettysburg and the other from his second inauguration, Lincoln joined with Reagan as a man also from humble beginnings. Both were born in the state of Illinois; both spent their early years memorizing the Bible and valued its contents, not only as truth but as a luminous and inspiring pattern for communicating. They shared a unique legacy and respect for language—its uses and its power.

CHAPTER TWO

The Source of His Bedrock Beliefs

It was a blazingly hot Washington, DC, autumn afternoon as we walked out of the Oval Office together, through the Rose Garden, and toward the presidential motorcade of twelve idling cars lined up on the South Lawn's circular driveway. Reagan took big strides, as if he were always wearing cowboy boots, which he didn't, and sort of glided wherever he was headed in a manly, graceful way.

Walking with him, as I was that day, I had to catch up to him all the time in the way that you walked with your dad when you were five years old. His shoes, which were refined and elegant but durable, always bore a perfect shine; although he had stewards to do the shining, I always imagined that shiny shoes were just a part of his identity even before he walked the White House grounds. His walk was a part of his communication. It was powerful. Speechwriter Peggy Noonan commented on this in her book *When Character Was King* when she wrote: "When I had begun working for Reagan, in 1984, I used to watch him from across the Rose Garden, or as he walked from the White House to the Old Executive Office Building, or as he bounded into the East Room for a luncheon. And what always struck me was his friendly grace, his enjoyment of the moment and of other people and his intuitive understanding of the presidential style. No one is ever trained to be President, and usually a President either walks in [to the White House] getting it or he doesn't. Some learn the role along the way, some never do. Reagan always comported himself as if he got it so easily, so effortlessly, that he didn't even notice that he had it."

By fall of 1981 we were ready to unveil the details of his Private Sector Initiatives program, and there was to be an initial rollout in New York and Washington. In New York, the President announced the initiative in the ornate and cavernous white-and-gold Waldorf Astoria ballroom, where the New York Partnership was meeting. The Partnership was founded by David Rockefeller and a group of business leaders who were helping finance the improvement of just about everything in New York City. This made the city a logical place to introduce a program that Reagan was passionate about and believed would improve the quality of life in every city, not just New York. But before the New York meeting took place, the first unveiling was held on October 5 in Washington, DC, at a national convention of the National Alliance of Business.

Our destination that unusually muggy Washington afternoon was the ballroom of the historic Sheraton Wardman Park Hotel, where the President would speak to an audience of several hundred conference attendees. While we waited for the motorcade to leave the White House grounds, there was a delay, possibly related to traffic control on the motorcade route up Connecticut Avenue over Rock Creek Park to the hotel, and as it was just the President and me in the backseat of the heavy, black-armored stretch Cadillac, we launched into conversation.

Using every minute of the delay, I started to review with the President what we would be accomplishing at the hotel event. I thought that was what a good presidential advisor should do. Reagan had a better idea. He had already been fully briefed about the schedule for the day by Dave Fischer, his very competent personal aide, so the President took over from me and explained just why he thought this program was so important. Of course we had thoroughly discussed the scope and goals of this initiative in talks at Camp David and in subsequent meetings, so I was not sure what new material he would cover during the car ride. But what he told me caught me by surprise. It turned out to be my Reagan education—an introduction to the roots and origins of his belief system—and it charted a course for me in understanding him that has been uniquely valuable ever since.

He began by telling me in detail and at length about his mother, Nelle. In fact, the major share of this conversation was about his mother. He described her work as a preacher called upon to substitute for the regular pastor at the Disciples of Christ Church—and at other churches in nearby rural Illinois towns where his family happened to be living in rental apartments and houses at the time. He told me that when he was a young boy, she read the Bible to him, and she actually had him read through it several times and required him to memorize key passages, then report to her on their meaning. He said that she had also practiced her sermons in front of him and asked him for his comments and critique, then took him with her when she was called to the pulpit. He also told me how she would take him along on her house calls to families in need of help, as well as take him on visits to jails to minister to the inmates and hospitals to visit the sick. Nelle would spring into action whenever she perceived there was a need in any family in their community, including making not only her own clothes but clothes for the indigents she ministered to. As the President continued talking, I could see that Nelle was his ideal and that she had been the most important person in his life.

As a one-time, aspiring small-town actress, Nelle also wrote morality plays, and she had her son perform in them. Nelle felt a calling not only to preach but also to minister to those less fortunate, to pray for them, and even to perform healings on them, which the President described to me. His mother took up sewing to make ends meet. He went on to tell me how impressed he was with her outreach, because in fact his family was about as poor as any of the others she ministered to.

I asked him if he had been troubled that his mother gave so much to others when his own family needed help. He said it was just a part of who she was, and he didn't seem to mind because she gave him enough attention and the tools to get by. He had to share his mother with others, and his family also had to share the meager assets of their life with other families as well. He said that while he admired his dad for certain things, such as his storytelling abilities, his father was a serious disappointment to him because of his alcohol problems. His mother, though, gave him a feeling of security because of her foundational principles, love of God, knowledge of the Bible, and desire to help people.

In what he told me I began to see the values that shaped him and took him to the highest office in the land. I could also see that among Nelle's virtues, which he explained continued long after he had left home and almost right up until the day she died, was self-denial. While Reagan had veered somewhat from that principle due to the requirements of his various public jobs, he never abandoned the idea that talking about one-self was somewhat sinful. That is why he used storytelling to deflect interest in him personally, and to shield himself from personal disclosure.

As I began to fit these pieces together, I later learned that Nelle had also given her eleven-year-old son, "Dutch" (as he was known growing up), a novel to read to help him cope with his dad's alcohol problems. This book was so profoundly influential and life changing for him that after reading it several times he announced he wanted to pattern his life after the young man featured in the book—a protagonist who actually went to Washington himself and entered national politics after coping with his own father's problems with alcohol. The more I learned about this book, the more I could also see that its moralistic thesis formed the model for much in Reagan's own policy playbook, including the very PSI program I was running. The book, *That Printer of Udell's*, was written by former Disciples of Christ pastor Harold Bell Wright, a proponent of practical Christianity and the theology of good works. This novel was a prism into the life and character Reagan created for himself.

For Reagan, this was not a book he read and then tossed on a bookshelf. It provided a blueprint for the life he wanted. He not only read it several times, he recommended it to others and even brought it to Washington when he was elected President all those years later. Reagan's life fits the pattern of some children of alcoholics who re-create themselves or establish new identities as a coping mechanism. Reagan found the main actor in this book was so admirable that he assumed the character's goals for himself as well as the character's ways of dealing with disappointment throughout a career in public service. This assumption on Reagan's part of the life of the book's protagonist included following the main character's eventual move into national politics. The protagonist worked in the community and in churches that helped the poor. Through helping others, the protagonist became a community leader and made his life an example. This was what Reagan strived to emulate, and after reading this book myself it was easy to discern the pattern Reagan followed—although Reagan's life had its own unique twists and turns. It is, however, how Reagan came to adopt the "servant" view of leadership.

Once I learned about this book and the role it played in Reagan's development, a light went off in my own mind. Now I could understand why he favored the PSI project and why it meant so much to him. I could also see why he took the time to explain his beliefs to me as the person responsible for managing, at that time, one of his signature achievements. PSI was his opportunity to bring to the forefront his personal beliefs about people helping people—from the ground up. This was one of the chief tenets in the Harold Bell Wright book that had such a big impact on this President. Reagan spoke of the Wright book throughout his life and returned to it at times to see how his life was shaping up relative to his role model, the protagonist in the book.

On that motorcade ride to the hotel, he went on to talk about how his mother continued her good works after she and his dad moved to California in retirement and into a home Reagan bought for them in Los Angeles—the first house they ever owned. He told me that he was impressed that no one had to tell her or even ask her to do it; she had an instinctive motivation to give to others. He saw this unselfishness as a typically American trait, and he wanted to magnify that and encourage others to follow her example. This virtuous woman whom he admired greatly was surely the most influential person in his life, and the qualities she expressed—her character, values, and faith—stuck with him for the rest of his life. Nelle was his rock, and her values became his values and helped him deal with an often-absent father and other challenges that he encountered throughout his life. He told me how he stuck to the beliefs that Nelle instilled in him, tried never to deviate from them, and they formed an ideal for him to adhere to. He was proud of the fact that he had never had a period in his life when he abandoned or rebelled against his upbringing in the church.

Nelle's activism and confident example also gave Reagan a respect and an ability to work with and have relationships with strong women. From the way Reagan talked about his mother in the car that day, I could see that she provided a safe harbor of stability for him as he grew up, which his father did not. Reagan found security in adopting her spiritual and religious beliefs, which were grounded in Bible teaching. He also mentioned to me something I have since read about in describing his home growing up: There was no prejudice, no racial comments allowed, no hatred toward anyone voiced in their household. Serious financial struggles, instability, and alcoholism were present in that house; however, because of Nelle's determination and faith, there was an unexpected optimism that, somehow, good would always and ultimately win out.

I think this was something Reagan just grabbed hold of and never let go. It was his own personal safe place of security, known only to him and rarely divulged to others. This attitude of optimism would not have appeared justified by the Reagans' circumstances and living conditions growing up. This revelation was what really interested me most. I knew Reagan was an optimist, and I had watched him handle the assassination attempt with an unusually positive attitude. However, at that time, I was uncertain about where this outlook, which sustained him even under the greatest challenges, came from. Now I knew.

Many U.S. Presidents have had exceptionally strong mothers who shaped the values of their sons. In fact, a majority of the Presidents who served in the twentieth century had this powerful influence, and they include (especially) Franklin Roosevelt, Harry Truman, John F. Kennedy, Jimmy Carter, Bill Clinton, both George Bushes, and Barack Obama. This motorcade conversation was not, of course, the first time Reagan had talked or written about his own mother and her influence on him, but this was the first time I was hearing it one-on-one. What he told me began to peel back his outer layer just enough and led to further conversations on the roots of this faith, ingrained spiritual perspective, and unshakable belief system. As personal a session as this was, it also had that impersonal feeling about it, because he was telling his story with both feeling and an objective distance at the same time. Some people would be emotional talking about their mothers. Reagan talked about her in respectful tones, as if she were in the car right with us, but his description was unemotional in tone—in keeping with this unique Reagan personality trait.

When I share this story with others, they usually respond with some surprise and perhaps also disbelief, because it opens up a new view of Reagan for them. His image suffered from not sharing enough about his actual personal beliefs as well as more about his quiet actions behind the scenes. On balance, however, rather than take the path of Jimmy Carter—who talked about his Christian beliefs, wrote church lessons, and taught Sunday

School while President—Reagan's silence did not necessarily represent what was going on inside the man. However, his need to keep these components of his personality wrapped up was probably, on balance, something that contributed to his being perceived as a strong leader rather than a vulnerable one and allowed him to not be marginalized politically for his beliefs.

When we reached the kitchen receiving dock of the hotel auditorium that humid afternoon, which was the most secure location the Secret Service could find for the arrival of the motorcade, he walked into the ballroom, was introduced, and began his speech. This was a speech I had seen and reviewed during the preceding week; however, I could now understand, for the first time, the principal reason he was considered an effective communicator. It was basically because he was genuinely talking about his own personal beliefs, as he did at other times, and that gave what he was discussing a passion, an authenticity, and an honesty that was felt by the audience.

This was what he did throughout most of the eight years of his presidency—talk, illustrate, and explain his undeviating and deeply held principles. That was it. He knew his subject as long as it related to the beliefs he brought into the White House in 1981. It may have been a speech about taxes, defense, public housing, or transportation—but his speeches were fundamentally about his personal beliefs and that is what made them believable. As Reagan's senior communications aide, David Gergen, explained it, "Reagan was eager that his tales illustrate the larger American story as he believed in it. They were a critical part of his connection with his followers—as critical as the values he emphasized. The two went together: The values informed the stories and the stories brought the values to life."

Let's look at a couple of key speeches in which Reagan artfully and more obviously used his beliefs to support specific policy objectives. For domestic policy, let's turn to his economic speech to Congress in 1981:

"The question is, are we simply going to go down the same path we've gone down before, carving out one special program here, another special program there? I don't think that's what the American people expect of us. More important, I don't think that's what they want. They're ready to return to the source of our strength.

"The substance and prosperity of our nation is built by wages brought home from the factories and the mills, the farms, and the shops. They are the services provided in ten thousand corners of America: the interest on the thrift of our people and the returns for their risk-taking. The production of America is the possession of those who build, serve, create, and produce.

"For too long now, we've removed from our people the decisions on how to dispose of what they created. We've strayed from first principles. We must alter our course.

"The taxing power of government must be used to provide revenues for legitimate government purposes. It must not be used to regulate the economy or bring about social change. We've tried that, and surely we must be able to see it doesn't work."

Reagan was a master of repetition. I think he hoped that if he could just state his principles frequently enough, they would be accepted and maybe even adopted by others as their own. Here in this speech about tax reform he is weaving in, as he did in almost all his speeches, what I call his "belief phrases" such as: "source of our strength," "legitimate government purposes," "first principles," and others, some of which were also drawn directly from the U.S. Constitution, which he revered. He also felt that if he could inspire people to subscribe to his personal point of view, he would galvanize, if not completely unify, the conservative political movement and what he considered to be, at that time, the fundamentally conservative outlook of a majority of Americans. First came his values and second the policy initiatives to build on them.

In the realm of foreign policy, his 1982 speech at the Palace of Westminster in London was a clear example of communicating from these beliefs:

"If history teaches anything, it teaches self-delusion in the face of unpleasant facts is folly. We see around us today the marks of our terrible dilemma—predictions of doomsday, antinuclear demonstrations, an arms race in which the West must, for its own protection, be an unwilling participant. At the same time we see totalitarian forces in the world who seek subversion and conflict around the globe to further their barbarous assault on the human spirit. What, then, is our course? Must civilization perish in a hail of fiery atoms? Must freedom wither in a quiet, deadening accommodation with totalitarian evil?

"Sir Winston Churchill refused to accept the inevitability of war or even that it was imminent. He said, 'I do not believe that Soviet Russia desires war. What they desire is the fruits of war and the indefinite expansion of their power and doctrines. But what we have to consider here today while time remains is the permanent prevention of war and the establishment of conditions of freedom and democracy as rapidly as possible in all countries.'

"Well, this is precisely our mission today: to preserve freedom as well as peace. It may not be easy to see; but I believe we live now at a turning point."

Here again, Reagan, the preacher, is using religious hints of Armageddon to inspire the listener based on his knowledge of the teaching of the end times. He also associates himself with Churchill, the great orator and leader, which was especially appropriate because this speech was delivered on British soil, and his own fight against the aggression of Soviet expansionism was not unlike the one Churchill saw and experienced with Nazism. Here Reagan's beliefs were framing the debate and shaping his communication.

What Were His Basic Core Beliefs?

So what then *were* Reagan's unique plain and simple beliefs, the ones that came through so clearly in every speech and gave heft and impact to his communication? I would sum them up in the following points—and these are taken directly from what he said himself, publicly and privately, over and over again, but they are my own interpretation. There may be others, but these are the ones that stand out to me in the life and communications of Ronald Reagan:

1. The universe was created and continues to be governed by a beneficent, loving, caring, redemptive, intelligent, and knowable God.
2. Man is made in His image, and therefore man's birthright is freedom, not domination.
3. God is accessible and compassionate; He hears our prayers and answers them.
4. Each human life is destined to be used by a Higher Power for His purpose.
5. Human governments must be designed, structured, maintained, and managed to be subordinate to the will of the people. Government gains its consent and power to govern from the people. When government keeps its

people from self-determination, it is evil. Government is servant, not master. Opportunity to improve human well-being is created primarily by the private sector in business and philanthropy, and in families, churches, and community organizations where people are helping people.

6. Man is inherently good and has a duty to care for his fellow man.

7. There is an inevitable march toward human progress and improvement. Anything is possible. Despite the disruption, war, and hatred that appear, mankind's best days always lie ahead. There is hope for the future.

8. America has a destiny and a responsibility to safeguard the freedoms and liberty that are the features of its Constitution and founding and to extend this freedom throughout the globe through democratic reforms.

9. To bring about the ultimate deterrence of war and conflict, strength, conviction, and solidarity are the best methods.

10. As a country founded upon ideals that protect and preserve individual liberty, America is the world's best and last hope. It is a "shining city on a hill." If this light grows dim, the rest of the world suffers.

Reagan, the communicator and leader, acquired his beliefs as a child, teenager, and young adult from the religious and other teachings of his mother and others in his community. He held on to them, tested them, put them to good use in his leadership and communicator roles, and never deviated from them. For him there would have been no definition for or direction to his leadership, and no inspiration, authenticity, meaning, or depth to his speeches without this foundation. Two-thirds of all his speeches are comprised of words that speak to these beliefs.

The question arises: Why does it matter what Reagan's personal principles were? If we want to know why Reagan is associated with strong and effective leadership, this is where we need to look—directly at his personally held beliefs. People come by their belief systems by inheritance, tragedy, struggle, happenstance, recruitment, education, or just plain trial and error, and today increasingly diverse and dynamic types of belief systems are not easy to navigate or to adopt. Reagan had a less difficult time in this department, because he adopted his beliefs early in life and kept the precepts and principles that were largely considered mainstream in American culture at the time of his youth and during his presidency.

CHAPTER THREE

Reagan, Focused and Self-Contained

A telling illustration about the resolutely unknown Reagan comes directly from my friend and seasoned journalist Susan Waters. When Susan was assigned by *W Magazine* to conduct a face-to-face personal interview with Reagan in the Oval Office, she asked her publisher, the venerable John Fairchild, for a good question to ask the President that might really draw out the inner Reagan, cover new ground, and make some news. Following his suggestion, she framed her question this way: "So Mr. President, can you tell me," Susan started cautiously, "knowing, as we all do, how much you enjoy spending long hours up at your California ranch clearing brush and doing other chores…what you really *think* about when you are chopping all that wood?" Her hope for something even slightly introspective and illuminating was dashed when, right on the uptick from her question, without missing a beat, came his response: "The wood!" Susan told me it took her a few moments to recompose herself and continue in the previous cadence of the interview and admit defeat at gaining any insight into the unknowable Reagan.

"The wood!" In two words Reagan had said nothing and

yet revealed everything about himself or, at least, what I think are three specific insights. First, that he was focused, single-minded, and fiercely determined to guard against saying anything casually introspective. Second, that by being focused he could be successful in simply cutting the wood. Third, that his mind was uncluttered and unfettered. Susan says she will never forget that session for what it did and did not reveal about her subject. This type of encounter adds an amount of mystery to the man.

Reagan was genuinely heartfelt, but he never opened up his heart in a vulnerable or personal way to the public. He was formal, courtly, and gentlemanly. What was more, he never suffered the type of personal embarrassments that sometimes force quiet private personalities to the surface in some presidencies and expose more of the peculiarities of the person residing in the presidential mansion. He never talked about his troubles as a way of creating personal sympathy, empathy, adulation, or attention, the way many politicians and celebrities have.

Often during my White House years, I felt that it was a failing on Reagan's part not to better define his character to the public. I thought to myself, time and again, if he did not speak up and explain himself, he would be permanently defined by a group of journalists and biographers who would make certain what the public knew about the fortieth President was what they wanted the public to know. Why the reticence? Why the silence on his part? In a way this was something both Reagan and his wife, Nancy, shared: They tightly controlled and managed who they were and to whom they would reveal themselves—that is, what they would reveal about their innermost thoughts and vulnerabilities. As far as I could find out after spending countless hours in Washington and traveling around the world with them, there was nothing earth-shattering to hide, no major demons to unleash. This was just their approach: to handle their public personas, or what today we might call their brand.

The President carried with him an air of mystery that came through to all but the most incurious observer. But then, mystery also makes public figures more alluring, more fascinating—although this is somewhat puzzling, considering the massive amounts of exposure to which celebrities subject themselves or even create about themselves. The ones who endure the exposure and become legends usually do carry an element of mystery about them.

This could be said, for example, about Abraham Lincoln, Franklin Roosevelt, or both President and Mrs. Kennedy, who tightly controlled their images and remain mysterious—although they were massively documented, endlessly analyzed, and frequently written about. Jacqueline Kennedy went so far in managing her brand as to never give a formal interview to a journalist. The only exception was her February 1962 televised tour of the White House with veteran journalist Charles Collingwood, which presented the picture she wanted in the way she wanted it in the most powerful building in the world. Following the assassination of her husband, she went on to further control the Kennedy brand by defining its one thousand days in office as a modern-day Camelot.

The Kennedys were proof that being on constant public display does not necessarily demystify a person. In terms of the potency of leadership, visibility does not necessarily equate with strength, and public familiarity does not always equal public confidence. There is also evidence that leaders who disappear from public view—even for a brief time, and especially during a crisis or controversy—and are not accessible to their constituents, suffer in public opinion as well. Reagan was there outwardly in plain sight every day of his presidency but often inwardly inaccessible.

Reagan, Religion, and Ego

As President, Reagan did not appear to the public as especially religious in a denominational or sectarian way—and that attitude may have actually seemed preferable to a majority of his constituents. After all, Americans elect a governmental and not a religious leader—although most have preferred that their leaders, in general, be at least prayerful people who know how to turn to a Higher Power in national crisis and who feel subordinate to it, if for nothing else than to check their ambitions and promote humility. If Reagan had to be placed in any religious institution as an adult, he certainly had a comfortable fit in the Presbyterian Church. He was on good terms with his minister, Donn Moomaw, the gregarious and towering former UCLA linebacker and pastor of the Bel Air Presbyterian Church, where Reagan was a member for three decades. In Washington his minister was the Reverend Louis Evans, a former Californian and the senior pastor at the National Presbyterian Church.

Reagan called upon Evans and his staff for special help several times during his terms in office, including for communion following the assassination attempt. Moomaw was also a frequent guest at the White House, and he offered prayers at both of Reagan's inaugurations.

Reagan used the presidential pulpit to dramatic effect to

share his beliefs but he was not pedantic or preachy. He delivered sermons—not in clerical robes but in the suit and tie of the layman. He left Sunday School teaching behind decades before when he departed his hometown of Dixon, Illinois.

Unlike most celebrities who have little to promote but their personalities, Reagan let his *im*personality define him. Reagan assumed the presidency; the presidency did not assume him. He signed on for a role and played it well. He stated often and to as many people who could hear it that he lived "above the store" and was only the temporary occupant of the house that also had been used by its previous tenants to good effect. These were both modest and self-effacing statements. Because he respected the Office of President to such a high degree, Reagan did not impose his personality on it; however, he did bring his robust belief systems to it, and he used this podium to trumpet his values.

Reagan was an evangelist for freedom, small government, individual liberty, and more, but he was not an evangelist for himself. He didn't need to be. The ideals he communicated were big enough. Therefore, Reagan rarely used the words *we* or *I* and frequently, neither of these pronouns in his speeches. Reagan did not practice this out of any strict adherence to grammatical tradition; it was his natural tendency not to seek credit for his ideas.

Reagan lived and breathed the hand-tooled, gold-embossed statement on the leather plaque he placed prominently at the front of his massive oak Oval Office desk: "There is no limit to what a man can do or where he can go, if he does not mind who gets the credit." By every test of his life and actions in the White House, Reagan followed this credo—even though the average person, despite being well intentioned, would have felt an instinctive desire to earn at least some credit. It didn't even register on Reagan's radar whether or not he received credit for his achievements. He was never credit-seeking or needy. Even though he worked in two of the most ego-driven industries— film and politics—Reagan seemed immune to this human trait or even to having a personal ego at all. When he was at the peak of stardom in motion pictures, he sought to downplay the female adulation promoted by the studio. The very fact that he also kept a second plaque on his desk that carried the message *It CAN be done* represents a personality that is both humble and bold at the same time, both self-deprecating and ambitious, his own rare combination of character traits.

There was no doubt that Reagan was competitive—but more with himself than with others. He had the determination and drive early in life to leave poverty and uncertainty behind and to attend college on a partial scholarship and make the football team—which for him was a serious mark of success—and then to advance in the broadcasting industry. Later he fought to be considered an accomplished actor. Far from passive, he wanted to excel and achieve but not necessarily from a point of personal vanity or to seek acclaim. He had the drive to win elections when urged by friends to run for governor; later, he thought he could do something good for the world in seeking the highest office. After some initial reticence, he also thought it was an ideal profession for someone like him.

We also know that his desire to achieve also came into play in a more unusual way, where there was a blending of human career planning and spiritual ambition. Early on while living in Dixon, Illinois, with his family, Reagan had even considered following the course of a close friend who was enrolling in divinity school—which could have resulted in an ordained

Reagan who might have ministered to hundreds. As it turned out, his sermons reached millions. His ultimate achievement was to play the dual role of political leader and spiritual evangelist at the same time. A review of all his speeches confirms this fact. At London's Guildhall, I sat to the right of the podium in the staff seats, which looked a lot like church pews, listening to a speech that could only be called a sermon. Here is some of what Reagan said:

"Ours is also a pilgrimage, a pilgrimage toward those things we honor and love: human dignity, the hope of freedom for all peoples and for all nations. And I've always cherished the belief that all of history is such a pilgrimage and that our Maker, while never denying us free will, does over time guide us with a wise and provident hand, giving direction to history and slowly bringing good from evil—leading us ever so slowly but ever so relentlessly and lovingly to a moment when the will of man and God are as one again."

It would not have been surprising to have heard those words as a part of an impressive sermon given in a church. But here was Reagan on a political and foreign policy platform sermonizing to the whole world when he also knew his words would be immortalized or at least frozen in the public record.

Then at the May 5, 1985, speech at the Bergen-Belsen concentration camp in Germany, where Anne Frank is buried, we heard Reagan sermonizing again:

"Everywhere here are memories—pulling us, touching us, making us understand that they can never be erased. Such memories take us where God intended His children to go—toward learning, toward healing, and, above all, toward redemption. They beckon us through the endless stretches of our heart to the knowing commitment that the life of each individual can change the world and make it better.

"We're all witnesses; we share the glistening hope that rests in every

human soul. Hope leads us, if we're prepared to trust it, toward what our President Lincoln called the better angels of our nature. And then, rising above all this cruelty, out of this tragic and nightmarish time, beyond the anguish, the pain and the suffering for all time, we can and must pledge: Never again."

This Churchillian approach to language and dramatic delivery are features rarely heard in speeches today. What Churchill and Reagan knew was that words were well invested in the minds and hearts of the audience when they had a purpose or an intention. Both men had felt a calling and a unique ability to lift the human spirit in order to achieve political results. Their words and dramatic delivery appealed to a higher human nature to dream, to achieve, and even, in Churchill's case, to survive. Not all speeches can be lofty, but a majority of theirs were. Some of Franklin Roosevelt's and John F. Kennedy's speeches achieve this dramatic spiritual liftoff as well.

Being highly self-contained, less vivid, and more controlled, Reagan has had less published in book form about him than many other Presidents. Twenty years after Reagan left office, a smaller number of major scholarly biographies had been written—not including the memoirs of Reagan aides and officials. Generally speaking, Presidents who have been associated with a big war, a scandal, or an economic depression tend to have attracted more writers to assess and relate them to the peaks and valleys in American history. Reagan did not have any of these especially dramatic defining peaks or valleys, although an economic recession figured largely in his first term, as did his focus on the Middle East and the Soviet Union.

According to public opinion polling, Reagan and Kennedy

are growing in popularity the farther away we get from their occupancy of the White House. According to Scott Farris, author of the intriguing and useful book *Kennedy and Reagan*, "The popularity of both men is actually increasing with time." When Gallup polled Americans on their greatest Presidents, the top vote getters were Lincoln, Reagan, and Kennedy— interestingly, these were also three of the most elusive and mysterious personalities in presidential history, and each was the target of an assassin. An ABC News survey found that "more respondents listed Lincoln as our greatest president... followed closely by Kennedy, with Reagan finishing fourth behind FDR... When a 2009 Gallup poll specifically matched Reagan and Kennedy against the three men historians typically rank as our greatest presidents—Washington, Lincoln, and FDR—Reagan and Kennedy outpaced all three."

Another Gallup poll found Reagan's retrospective job approval rating to be an enviable 74 percent, which is higher than recent past Presidents, although during the eight years of his presidency it averaged 53 percent. These numbers may reflect the image of the man related to contemporary events or continued media presence. The sheer volume of media visibility of President Kennedy, partly the result of his assassination and the continuing controversy surrounding it, contributes significantly to his standing today. There are still millions of people living who were alive during both the Kennedy and Reagan presidencies, and their views of these men also register in any poll. While I cannot speak for Kennedy, I know that if Reagan were here watching the scene today, he would be as surprised and as unaffected by a rise in his popularity as he would have been in life.

The Assassination Attempt, His Health, His Appearance

An opportunity did arise to provide the public with more personal texture to Reagan right after the assassination attempt on March 30, 1981. This was when we learned about his ability to forgive his assassin and his use of humor while lying on a gurney being wheeled into the hospital operating room. Even in this extreme adversity, closer to death than the White House press secretary was authorized to report, he would not describe his suffering to the hospital staff beyond what the doctors needed to know from him. He deflected personal attention. He might have been fearful inside, but his eternal optimism dominated, and that was all he was willing to show the public. While I am certain that a terribly shaken Nancy Reagan, standing by his side in the hospital, did not find humor in it herself, Reagan famously quipped for the world "Honey, I forgot to duck" and "I sure hope the surgeon is a Republican" from his bed at the George Washington University Hospital emergency room. His dogged view that good would somehow ultimately trump evil gave him the ability to help the rest of the world deal with this tragedy. Reagan's mettle as a standard-bearer was being tested from his own hospital bed.

Reagan's apparent ability to forgive his would-be assassin, John Hinckley, provided another way to read his character. His Teflon personality had not stopped the bewildering intent of a deranged young man or the delivery of a bullet to his body, but it did stop this crime from complicating Reagan's view of his mission—in fact, as adversity often does, it clarified it. Of his forgiveness of Hinckley, Reagan later recounted:

"Yes [I forgave him] . . . I added him to my prayers that, well, if I

wanted healing for myself [then] . . . maybe he should have some healing for himself."

Reagan's daughter Patti Davis wrote that her father had told her that *"I know that my healing depends on my forgiving him [Hinckley]."* Pastor Louis Evans recounted in 2004 that when he went to give communion to Reagan at the White House after the shooting, the President told him about being in the hospital and said, *"I was really struggling and I didn't know if I would make it. God told me to forgive Hinckley. And I did. I forgave him. And immediately I began to breathe better."* I remember the discussion fostered by Reagan that he would meet with Hinckley face-to-face to forgive him. That was eventually ruled out by the perpetrator's doctors as possibly too disturbing for the troubled young man.

On July 13, 1985, Reagan underwent cancer surgery. I happened to be the only senior staff person with him when he was being prepared for the procedure at Bethesda Naval Hospital in suburban Washington. My five-year-old daughter had painted him a little picture of some clouds and a rainbow, hoping to cheer him up (as if Reagan, the eternal optimist, needed cheering up), adding the line, "I love you. XXOO Claire." Reagan and I talked briefly about the surgery he was facing, then I reached into my pocket and gave him the picture. He looked at it for a minute and, despite being called by the doctors to be rolled into the operating room, said, "Jim, would you please hand me a piece of my personal stationery?" I was not sure what he wanted to do with the pale-green-hued gold-embossed paper, which was for use only by the President, but I watched him write: *"Dear Claire, Thank you very much for my card. You were very nice to think of me and I'm grateful. I love you too. Sincerely, Ronald Reagan."* He signed it and asked me to give it to my daughter.

A few minutes later, I walked alongside the rolling hospital bed halfway down the hall toward the operating room. Then I turned to leave the hospital, not realizing what awaited me. When I pushed open the swinging doors, there was the full White House and international press corps—and I mean hundreds of cameras and writers—all lined up and champing at the bit for personal anecdotes and factual information about the President's spirits and mood as he entered the operating room.

Finally I was confident I could offer them some real insight into the man. While I left medical details to the doctors and legal Constitutional matters (regarding temporary transfer of power to the Vice President while the President was under anesthesia) to the White House Counsel, I reported on his alertness and positive frame of mind. I also shared the little story about his letter writing to Claire, which in turn was widely reported in the media around the world. This added some much-needed color to his personality and to the way the public viewed him.

The next day I caught another small but poignant glimpse of the inner Reagan. For some reason the President had not planned a change of clothes for his return to the White House following his stay at Bethesda. Again I was in his room, and he asked me if I would mind returning to the family quarters in the White House to pick out an outfit for him to wear when he left the hospital the next day. Of course I went straight out to the White House motor pool, which was positioned right outside the hospital, jumped into one of the navy blue Chrysler sedans standing by, and was driven the nine miles back to 1600 Pennsylvania Avenue.

When I arrived, I went directly upstairs to the family quarters and to his dressing room and closet. This area spanned the space between the First Couple's large bedroom, with its hand-painted bird mural wallpaper, and a room that he used as his at-home office. This office was where the Reagans also ate supper on folding tables and watched TV—on the rare evenings when they were not hosting an event on the State Floor or traveling outside Washington.

The closet was uncluttered and the clothes were few. There, to my surprise, I found the personal possessions of a very simple man.

Yes, of fine tailoring and quality, but not extravagant in number. There was a black suit, a brown suit, a blue suit, two plaid suits. One brown belt, one black belt. One pair of shoes in each color with the accessories you would imagine—but not lavish or fashionable in any way. I stood quietly in front of the open closet for a few minutes to assess what I was seeing and think to myself, "Here is the leader of the free world who to all outward appearances is a man of wealth and substance, and yet it looks like he is actually unencumbered by the material necessities of life and not at all like how he is being portrayed by the media or understood by the public." I could see that Reagan was a man of simple Midwestern tastes—sartorially and otherwise. He was not acquisitive, but he knew what he wanted and did not buy an item more.

Then I remembered my task and quickly picked out a casual shirt, trousers, socks, shoes, and so on among the simple options I had. I took them back to the hospital, still trying to grasp what I had seen about the man from this minor domestic but insightful task.

One time I suggested to the President that he could look younger if he would start wearing shirt collars higher on his neck to cover some of the sagging signs of aging. He agreed to try my plan, and I went out to buy him a new shirt for a trial run, along with a new burgundy-and-gray-striped tie. I bought both on approval from a friendly but unknowing sales-man at Britches of Georgetowne, my own favorite Washington men's store. The salesman must have assumed I was buying this shirt for my dad when I asked for a sixteen-and-a-half-inch neck size—he knew I wore an inch smaller.

The next day I left it for the President upstairs in the family quarters with a note. I thought he would just try it out and let me know what he thought of it. After several days of expect-ing to see him appear with this new, more youthful look, I was disappointed because he had not said anything about my purchase, and so I finally asked him what had happened.

"Jim," he said, not disingenuously, "I really tried it out and wanted it to work, but the collar was so high up and tight on my neck, and I was so unaccustomed to it, that I just could not change my old habits. I like the way mine hangs down lower on my neck. It's just more comfortable that way. Thanks, but could you just return the shirt?"

The shirt went back, but I noticed that he did not return the tie. Later I realized that he wore that particular tie over and over again on more occasions than others, and he reflected on it in a personal letter he sent me. I guess it just suited him, and it was appropriately conservative and presidential.

Reagan was a creature of habit, and he didn't think he needed a youthful appearance to impress anyone or to improve his polling numbers. He dressed appropriately and confidently, and it engendered confidence in return from his constituents and peers. He dressed with respect for the occasion. There was no question that Reagan wanted to dress the part, and he did, but clothes were a prop for him and not something about which he thought a great deal.

He especially liked wearing blue jeans and cowboy boots.

One evening when the Reagans hosted a barbeque on the South Lawn for members of Congress and their families, he and I both emerged from the family quarters in blue jeans. Reagan got a kick out of that, later writing to me, *"The White House can be fun if you dress for it."*

I remember one evening as we were preparing to leave for a state visit abroad—a trip of about ten days. I was in the family quarters as the racks of the Reagans' clothing were about to be transported to the belly of Air Force One for an early-morning departure from Andrews Air Force Base. I saw long racks of the First Lady's clothes in carefully labeled dress bags, and then I turned to the President and urged him to finish packing his own clothes so that the military aides could get everything out to the plane that night. He was sitting in his study in one of the two red-flowered armchairs in front of his desk, reading the heavy black spiral-bound briefing books prepared by the National Security Council and the State Department for the trip. The door was open to the yellow-carpeted cross hall a few feet away, and he answered me by pointing over to the end of the clothes rack and said, "Oh, Jim, I finished packing a long time ago, and if you look over there you will see the results. That's my bag at the end."

So I went to make sure everything was there. Much to my astonishment, at the very end of the long line of the First Lady's dresses and suits was, by comparison, a very thin and compact suit bag for his clothes—just what was needed and not a piece more. A couple suits and precisely just the right number of shirts and ties. I always thought that his compact packing reflected his compact and contained personality. He knew in absolute terms what he needed, and he packed it for himself. There was no indecision.

Reagan, Family Values, and Family Substitutes

Early in the Administration, in mid-1981, I wrote a "Family Values" memo to Mike Deaver, the keeper of the Reagan brand, who along with Nancy Reagan performed well as a team—not unlike the Arthur Schlesinger–Jacqueline Kennedy partnership that created the myth of Camelot to burnish the Kennedy era. In my memo, I suggested to Mike that we needed to show the Reagans in a more family-friendly way, talking about family values and bringing more families in to the White House—even if they didn't have the name Reagan.

Mike, the one person who knew them best, looked askance at my suggestions and said these ideas would never work because they would not be authentic. "The Reagans can't talk about the perfect family when they don't have one, and furthermore, bringing it up would only shine a spotlight on this situation," he told me plainly.

I was frankly disappointed by his reaction, because I thought this would help Americans more easily identify with the Reagans. But I was wrong. In the same way, I had mistakenly urged Nancy Reagan to be photographed in the upstairs family kitchen with an apron on—even though she had never cooked a meal in her life, as she quickly informed me, putting an end to my photographic scheme. By this time she and Mike were teaching me valuable lessons about authenticity and how it is communicated, and I was their student.

During my time in the White House, there was a persistent natural desire on the part of the media to know everything about the President and First Lady—to really give them a public identity with more texture and controversy. There were several reasons for this. The Reagans were relatively unknown in Washington at the time of the 1980 election, and their arrival was preceded by a number of unflattering news stories about them from California-based and other political writers.

On the nonpolicy side of communications—equally as important as the policy side—we suffered from not having the idealized picture of a traditional family with kids at the White House. As a result I was one of a small group of senior advisors who proposed a simple though not completely satisfying solution: a dog! It is plain and simple to see that throughout the history of the presidency, photographers and chroniclers of the White House and its tenants favor kid stories and family gatherings. Kids help define the character of the White House and its residents, and we lacked this fundamental element to make a perfect stage set. We had only two adults instead of a typical American family with kids. The Reagan children were adults and out on their own, and they valued their independence and privacy—neither of which they were fully accorded. This was difficult territory for the Reagans.

With the exception of Maureen, Reagan's ebullient and politically active daughter with Jane Wyman, in whom the media did not really take a great deal of interest, her siblings rarely came around and never moved in, as did so many presidential children in previous administrations. Maureen could often be found staying in the Lincoln Bedroom for long stretches of time when she was working at the Republican National Committee or heading the United Nations Decade of Women's Conference in Africa. Maureen's brother, Michael, who appeared to me to be a good-natured and wonderfully supportive son, was scarcely seen at the White House. The Reagans' other children, Ron and Patti, were mostly known for not agreeing with their father's political positions and could not be counted on frequently enough to provide a loving backdrop of support except at Christmas. These were essentially good kids and good parents who came into the White House with family baggage. So we started looking for dogs. After all, the Roosevelts, Kennedys, Johnsons, and Nixons all had dogs during their tenure.

The first Reagan dog was a Bouvier des Flandres who grew bigger and bolder than we had anticipated. While training by the Usher's Office was in earnest, Lucky, as he was called, was not interested in being a lapdog—unless you like your lap filled with eighty pounds of wiry feistiness. Lucky's antics were hilarious, and they satisfied photographers and writers—*for a while*. This would not last long, however, and soon Lucky was taken to the ranch to live out his days watching beautiful views of the sunset high in the Santa Ynez Mountains above Santa Barbara. Later, the dog vacancy was filled with a more house-friendly King Charles spaniel named Rex. This dog was not seen as much by the public, and our experiment largely fizzled. The point, which was conceded at that moment, was that leaders need to provide human interest elements for the media to help define them. Kids, dogs, sportsmanship, the arts, presidential vacations—all help paint a complete picture of the life of the leader and reveal more of the texture of their inner personalities. The Reagan family did not help in any of these categories.

Reagan, Friendly but Alone

During my many trips to California with the Reagans, I had occasional lunches in the Paramount Pictures commissary with the legendary producer A. C. Lyles, one of the President's oldest friends and the longest employed studio executive on the back lot at Paramount. He told me, "Ronnie was somewhat of a loner in Hollywood, always impersonal; but he was adept at making friends because of his sunny disposition. He stood out because of his almost courtly manners and gentlemanly appeal...and yet he always deflected personal interest in him by telling jokes and stories, and as a result he always had a little crowd around him. He had sort of an aura about him, and you knew he stood for something even then. You could tell he was different—in a good way." Lyles was especially helpful to me during those conversations. He educated me about the Reagans. He provided me with valuable insights about who they really were, how they lived, the problems they had with their children, and what motivated them—all based on what he had seen about them and their family from their long acquaintance over many decades.

During his film industry days, Reagan had purposefully honed his skills in telling the public what he wanted them to hear and know about him—and this is a skill still practiced by many successful film stars. By the time he entered politics, he knew what he would reveal of a personal nature (not much), what he was willing to share (even less), and what he felt was effective and required for the public to know about him (slim). During their White House years, the Reagans continued to court certain gossip columnists who had what they considered to be a sympathetic and politically useful attitude toward them and their personalities.

It took me (a person who had been brought up to think of gossip as sinister) a long time to understand this. I could see them repeating a pattern from their film careers: They courted the media, who wrote about their personal life, without having to reveal too much inwardly or be challenged outwardly. These interactions usually led certain writers to report candidly about Reagan's charm, sincerity, intelligence, and sense of fun. But beyond what Reagan shared with these columnists, there was an enigmatic nature to him that they were not terribly interested in anyway. Even his own wife, Nancy, wrote, "There's a wall around him. He lets me come closer than anyone else, but there are times when even I feel that barrier."

In my personal, one-on-one interactions with the President, he was unfailingly kind, jovial, appreciative, gentlemanly, interested, earnest, compelling, energetic, generous, and focused. However, he was never really personal—even in phone calls he made to me. I observed that this was also how he treated others—many of whom had worked for him far longer and knew him much better. Reagan could proffer my wife the most kind and caring glance and the most charming conversation and personally write my daughter the most meaningful and heartfelt letter, but when you left his presence you knew he wasn't thinking about you—he wasn't engaged in your life.

Here was the residue and effect of his boyhood, resulting in a character trait I finally realized was one of the most critical, yet generally unrecognized and underappreciated factors in his becoming a commanding global leader. Few have it— this unique impersonality or invulnerability to personal pique or ego. If he did have one, his ego was invisible to outsiders. He had isolated a part of his personality from the threat of disappointment in childhood, and as a result he did not clutter his mind with other people's business or what they thought of him. He was sympathetic toward people who were suffering, as illustrated in his personal letters and modest donations to those in trouble, but he always kept a safe distance from them.

I would have thought the public would be able to gauge the man by his words alone, but some found those too formal and Reagan too scripted. However, in the case of President Reagan, the "script" or his speeches and the mind of the man were in almost perfect harmony, and that was a part of the genius of his communication ability. But the media wanted, justifiably I thought, a more unscripted and casual acquaintance with him, and because they were largely denied this, they were suspicious and skeptical. I remember someone from the White House press office bounding into my office one day and exclaiming, "When are they [the Reagans] going to stop acting out a role and just be the President and First Lady?" Quietly I thought to myself: "I hope never—because they are doing a great job of it."

The *actor* label never left him, and it was used derisively by his opponents to imply that an actor is less intellectually or morally equipped to be President than, for example, a lawyer—which so many Presidents (and not all great ones) have been. Though Reagan was famous with his generation for having starred in movies, the fact was his résumé included many more jobs than just appearing in films—all of them preparing him for and leading up to his ultimate starring role as President.

Reagan was President for eight years, but the world was never on intimate terms with him. The world never owned a little bit of him as it has some other leaders who have lived out their personal lives in public. He made many of us feel better and more secure about our own lives but we were never invited into his. According to Fouad Ajami of Stanford University, "The Reagan presidency was about America, and never about Ronald Reagan."

That has a high-minded ring to it and may well be true; however, after his two terms were over, we were left with a lingering desire to know more than just biographical data about the man who dared Mr. Gorbachev to tear down the Berlin Wall, the man who was able to forgive his would-be assassin, John Hinckley, on the spot and live to tell about it. The world had to understand who Reagan was as a leader and communicator by what he said and did on a world stage and not from learning about his deeply private personal character, which he sheltered.

Reagan's success as a public leader was built on his private beliefs, and these gave him the ability to lead on the biggest stage. In speech after speech as President, Reagan offered the public a big dose of literary allusions and specific references to his spiritual and patriotic beliefs, but these quotations represented more than convenient elegance, artfully embedded in speeches by hopeful and extraordinarily talented speechwriters. For an American President, Reagan employed a significantly higher-than-average and exceptional use of Biblical and other classical writings and sayings in his speeches. This device worked especially well for him because these sayings represented what was actually embedded in his mind and heart and were not just gimmicks to be used to impress an audience, score a point, or win a vote.

For example, when Reagan, at the end of every televised Oval Office speech to the nation, signed off with "God Bless America," many viewers felt that Reagan *wanted* God to bless America. The reason they would have felt that was precisely because Reagan *did* want his country to be blessed by a Higher Power and that he himself prayed for this outcome. It was his own benediction to what was more often like a sermon than a speech—delivered from the big, old, carved oak desk that had also been used by John F. Kennedy. Reagan felt the gravity of his office and he respected it. It could be said that he belonged to his friend Jimmy Stewart's school of virtues, in which one lived life in this order: (1) love of God; (2) love of family; (3) love of country. This was what was working on the inside of the man. Reagan was not a placid, insensitive person. He was just afraid of letting people (including even some family members) too close to feel what he felt.

CHAPTER FOUR

The Global Evangelist

Reagan, the gifted communicator, was a speechwriter's dream. Every public presentation resulted from a team effort between the President and the writers—neither would have been quite as successful without the other. Reagan had high expectations for his White House staff of writers and received extraordinary results from them. They were the ones who could really get into the soul of the man better than anyone else on the President's staff. They often mined his own handwritten earlier writings for direction and stories, then followed his guidance, edits, and outlines carefully. He provided direction, inspiration, editing, and, finally, brilliant execution. He delivered the goods. He made the written word come alive.

Tony Dolan, the longtime and gifted Reagan speechwriter, said that "closer historical scrutiny of Reagan's writing before the presidency, as well as the extent of his involvement in his presidential speeches, has revealed that he was more than merely a great communicator but also a man of ideas, a cerebral president." Josh Gilder, another gifted writer for Reagan, commented that "Reagan's presence was just—I don't know— remarkable. We'd go in there all worked up over staff wars or the way the researchers weren't doing their work. We might even have been worked up over something important for a change, like the Sandinistas or the situation in the Middle East. Then Reagan would calm us right down. He was sweet and serene."

Many Presidents, especially George Washington, Abraham Lincoln, Thomas Jefferson, and John Adams, had used Biblical references, allusions, and quotations from inspired writers and thinkers liberally during their tenures. But we would have to go back to our first President and our sixteenth to find the same frequency with which the Bible was used in speeches given by the fortieth President. In *The God Strategy*, Kevin Coe and David Domke concluded that Reagan "altered the nature of religion and politics in America." They found that until Reagan, Presidents had mentioned God in an average of 46 percent of all the speeches they gave. Reagan's God and Bible references increased to a whopping 96 percent of all his speeches. As the critically important biographer Paul Kengor has written, Reagan's faith was "fundamental to a presidency that, in Ronald Reagan's mind, was undergirded by something far more profound than mere politics." One reviewer of Reagan's autobiography noted, "*An American Life* is filled with religious references. Time and again Reagan mentioned his deep trust in God and his frequent recourse to prayer."

Why did this work for Reagan on a global stage? No other world leader at the time, with the exception of his ally Pope John Paul II, was speaking quite like Reagan. Why was he not at all reticent to so frequently employ parables, stories, and quotations from the Bible, as well as from great and classical patriots, thinkers, writers, and poets? One simple answer is that these were features of good speechwriting, and they effectively and eloquently supported important points he was trying to make. During his time in office, the Bible was more frequently referred to and studied in schools—even as literature if not for religious purposes. More people, then, were familiar with its time-honored teachings whether they were religious or not. These references worked exceptionally well for Reagan, because he was not only inspired himself by the quotations he was reciting and believed in, but it was a convincingly *impersonal* way for him to define himself *personally*. If you seek Reagan, here is where you will find him—right in the Biblical and patriotic quotes he used over and over again.

When he quoted from or referred to the Bible—which he did in almost every speech—it was as if he were speaking in the third person and partnering with the prophets and apostles whom he was quoting. This was an effective communication device that gave him the opportunity to shine by borrowed light. His references to these great ideas and thinkers made his speeches glisten. Moreover, in so liberally quoting from the Bible, he was talking with old friends, and he was in familiar territory, because he was a Bible student himself and familiar with the material—conceptually, practically, and literally. Again, if you want to get to know Reagan, just accept what he said on the public platform, through the voices of individuals he quoted, as the best and most accurate characterization of him.

Perhaps more significant, what we see happening through Reagan's continual use of these Biblical references, as well as quotations from secular giants, was somewhat like an engineered construction project. He was laying the groundwork for a larger message that could sustain the specific foreign and domestic policy initiatives that would follow—and once people knew the overall design philosophy, they were ready for the specific engineering specifications. The building of the "message bridges" deployed by Reagan was in parallel to the policy developments going on to promote an effective Reagan doctrine at the State Department, the National Security Council, and especially the Pentagon, as well as other Cabinet agencies—and it paved the way for them oratorically.

Reagan was the standard-bearer, the advance guard. As early as his days as Governor of California, the media took notice of this element in him—of laying out a specific purpose based on values and then introducing his new policy proposals that pragmatically and thematically stemmed from these principles. *Newsweek* magazine even surprisingly described Reagan's view of himself during those days as "God's instrument." I am sure few of their readers knew what to make of this observation or knew what to do with it in their assessment of him as a leader.

A specific example of the relationship between the bridge-building goals embedded in the broad themes in his speeches and of resulting policy was his plan of action for disarming communism and ending the Cold War. In this work, he was an effective strategist who was methodically and patiently building his case for the ultimate defeat of what he considered an inhumane ideology. During his first term and early in his second term, his growing knowledge and understanding of the Russian people and Russian culture and history, as distinct from the Soviet state, convinced him that they were really a peace-loving, God-fearing people despite the domination of the atheistic, all-powerful bureaucracy. This knowledge, at times quite distinct from the advice offered to him through officials in the foreign policy apparatus, gave him the confidence to assertively speak to the evils of the Soviet system every chance he had—despite the pushback and criticism he fielded from official quarters. Once he acquired this deeper and broader understanding about the Russian people, he was, in some respects, his own man when it came to what he would say about U.S.-Soviet relations and when he would say it.

This, of course, concerned people who thought they knew far more than Reagan did about the region and its future, and they ridiculed him for it—and this even included some in his own political party. In many ways they did know more; it was just not the knowledge Reagan thought would be useful to him in pursuing his own personal conquest over evil. Reagan ultimately proved them wrong at times by keeping his own counsel and running with his own instincts, which were fueled by what I believe he thought of as his mission or calling in life. This was brought into a more vivid focus after he survived the assassination attempt.

In his job as President, the biggest role of Reagan's life, storytelling was no longer just a device to deter interest in him personally but was a way to soften the often muscular and assertive rhetoric he sometimes used in domestic and for-eign relations, and a way to charm—and perhaps warm up—a relationship, or even start one. Reagan had his own seemingly unending arsenal of stories, and this was generously added to by friends and speechwriters over the years. Mike Deaver told me that his personal goal was to provide Reagan with one new story or joke every day. He took this so seriously you could find him on a constant hunt for new material. Reagan was a good customer, because he would roar at a joke or funny story, and for the serious ones he could be easily moved with emotion. Deaver was rarely deterred from offering Reagan an off-color story, either. Reagan relished those even though they could not be retold in public. In fact, his appetite for a good story created a sort of gridlock of people lining up to win Reagan's favor by telling him one in hopes he had not already heard it before. I always felt insecure every time I was with the President alone and failed to use the opportunity to make him laugh through a good story. Nancy Reagan also jumped into the game. I remember listening to her on the phone with Mort Sahl, one of the most prolific comedians of the day, collecting stories—which she passed along to the President.

While both the Reagans loved to laugh, to entertain, and to be entertained, the President didn't use storytelling just to entertain but most often to make a point, paint an illustration, or stake a position—in a nonthreatening but educational way—by letting someone else, the characters in the story, do the instructing. His use of this type of storytelling is legendary and often compared to the skill in telling parables—a gift from his mother, Nelle, the substitute lay preacher, and also from his dad, who had a bit of the Irish storyteller in him. An example of his use of parable can be found in the famous 1988 Guildhall speech, in which he used the story on which the famous film *Chariots of Fire* was based to illustrate the unbreakable bond between America and Great Britain:

"It's a story about the 1920 Olympics and two British athletes: Harold Abrahams, a young Jew whose victory . . . was a triumph for all those who have come from distant lands and found freedom and refuge here in England; and Eric Liddell, a young Scotsman, who would not sacrifice religious conviction for fame. In one unforgettable scene, Eric Liddell reads the words of Isaiah. 'He giveth power to the faint, and to them that have no might, he increaseth their strength, but they that wait upon the Lord shall renew their strength. They shall mount up with wings as eagles. They shall run and not be weary.'

"Here, then, is our formula for completing our crusade for freedom. Here is the strength of our civilization and our belief in the rights of humanity. Our faith is in a higher law. Yes, we believe in prayer and its power. And like the Founding Fathers of both our lands, we hold that humanity was meant not to be dishonored by the all-powerful state, but to live in the image and likeness of Him who made us.

"More than five decades ago, an American President told his generation that they had a rendezvous with destiny; at almost the same moment, a Prime Minister asked the British people for their finest hour. This rendezvous, this finest hour, is still upon us. Let us seek to do His will in all things, to stand for freedom, to speak for humanity. 'Come my friends,' as it was said of old by Tennyson, 'it is not too late to seek a newer world.'"

I personally encountered the powers of Reagan's illustrative storytelling at the first official White House event I planned and presided over in 1981. It was a breakfast meeting in the Old Family Dining Room, the one rarely seen by the public, directly north of the much grander State Dining Room and facing Lafayette Park. This room was decorated in a regency yellow color and was often used as a serving pantry for state dinners and formal receptions—although it was a handsome and elegant room on its own. The guests included about thirty-five corporate and philanthropic foundation CEOs and community leaders.

After breakfast, Reagan started his remarks with a story about a very rich yet miserly old man who would never give anything to charity. He was visited one day by a delegation of a dozen or so community leaders who were urging him to become philanthropic—as the town's United Way Campaign needed donations. Reagan continued:

"The old miser said, 'And does the record show that I have an invalid

sister and bedridden brother, and that my mother is in an institution and that my father is near death in the local hospital?' Then an embarrassment filtered through the demanding guests who felt chastised that they had even come to press their neighbor for a donation at this time in his life, and they wanted to spring for the front door and escape. But the old man stopped them and, to their astonishment, went on to exclaim: 'I never gave them any money, so why should I give you any?' "

That story brought the house down, but it also left an indelible picture of general shame that comes of not being philanthropic—the whole point of the breakfast meeting being to promote more giving and stir up more philanthropic activism. Reagan won the day, as he usually did, and this time through a humorous but meaningful parable.

Instead of focusing on himself when speaking publicly, Reagan always turned the spotlight on his audience. He usually honored them—proving the truth of the adage: "People will like you better if you tell them their virtues rather than their faults." His love of America and his faith in Americans was often answered with respect from many of his fellow citizens of all political persuasions, and they often included the voices of those who disagreed with him politically and even disliked him personally. Reagan wanted his presidency to be not so much about him but about the country he served, its prosperity, its growth, its character, and its role in promoting free and democratic societies across the globe. It was on this basis that he launched his eight-year evangelistic tour promoting a view of the world as he saw it—governed by a Higher Power, with good ultimately prevailing over evil, and where men can live in peace and in freedom in law-abiding, democratic societies that protect the rights and freedom of the individual.

Reagan's Primary Spiritual Orientation

Reagan was a Sunday School teacher early in his life. In fact, even while a college student, he drove from Eureka College—itself a church-affiliated college—every weekend one hundred miles back to his hometown of Dixon, Illinois, to teach teenage classes at the First Christian Church. He didn't just substitute-teach or fill in when it was convenient—he never missed a Sunday. It is surprising to many people to learn that Reagan had even taught Sunday School at all. It took an adventuresome biographer to unearth this fact years later, because Reagan rarely, if ever, talked about it once he reached Washington. In fact, though he was criticized for it, he rarely even went to church while in office and didn't really seem to need church services—although on occasion he said that he wished he could be like a regular parishioner and be a part of a religious service. After the assassination attempt, increased security measures were in place, and visiting unsecured venues such as churches proved to be problematic; so, it was generally ruled out by the scheduling committee on which I served, and by Nancy Reagan herself—who was always fearful about her husband going anywhere that was difficult to secure.

To truly understand what made this enigmatic man, the fortieth President of the United States, tick requires something out of the ordinary. In order to define him accurately we have to shift our point of reference away from a strictly political context. Once we do that, we see a man who was basically and primarily spiritually minded or faith oriented; and by that I mean that he was a man motivated in everything he did by his overriding personal relationship with his God.

Without this perspective of Reagan's character, it is impossible to understand him and how and why he accomplished what he did during his eight years in national political office. This wasn't just a segment or isolated compartment of his personality; his faith was the overwhelming influence on his thinking and actions. It was just the plain fact of how he developed as a human being—enormously influenced by his earlier days under the tutelage of his very religious and virtuous mother.

While an orientation to faith or a profession of faith is not uncommon for political leaders, for Reagan it was not an occasional dip into prayer on an as-needed basis. He did not dial up God as a crisis was about to occur and ask for divine intervention. Stated simply, it meant he lived life largely from a spiritual viewpoint rather than a human one. Through this lens he saw not only his own life but history as well—and this view grew even clearer, stronger, and deeper during his two terms.

I believe he did march to a different drummer than do most politicians, following the direction of a very specific voice familiar to him and rooted in his convictions, but not necessarily heard by those around him including his friends and family, officials, and advisors. There is an abundance of evidence to support the theory of his faith orientation, including the fact that his first twenty-three years of life were spent entirely in and around a church that stressed an applied Christianity based on a thorough understanding of Biblical truth and an active faith through good works. While he was growing up, the church was the principal frame of reference around which his life revolved. Those were his most important formative and grounding years. Some teenagers deviate from or at least test their religious upbringing and training. There is no evidence that Reagan ever did. He continued a strong commitment to his faith throughout his college years, including attending a church-affiliated school and being personally mentored by his pastor—who also happened to be the father of his longtime girlfriend, whom he expected to marry.

His diaries also detail and support this view with entries explaining why he was skeptical of and sometimes at odds with his government advisors. He would not compromise his values, although he would on occasion compromise purely on policy or legislative initiatives as necessary to reach political accommodation. From his spiritual perspective, the world was black and white. From his political perspective, there were shades of gray. This blend is how he made it work—how he must have justified compromise. Accepting this premise is indispensable to dissecting and understanding the quiet man often unreachable to those around him. When he was widely quoted—after the assassination attempt—as saying that he would devote the balance of his life to whatever Divine Providence wanted him to do, I believe that he was stating something that he had always felt about himself and his mission. It was just a convenient time for him to say it, and the assassination attempt also made it more poignant.

Suzanne Massie, the author of the classic book on Russia, *Land of the Firebird*, and Reagan's personal, nongovernmental advisor on Russian culture from 1983 to 1987, remarked that in her seventeen almost exclusively one-on-one sessions with Reagan, he mostly listened, absorbed, probed, and then questioned. This made her somewhat uncomfortable, because she had to do most of the talking. Then when he had absorbed the details of the briefings she conducted, and compared them with the briefings he was receiving on Soviet affairs from official U.S. government sources, he would discuss the action he wanted to take. Once he reached this position and was ready to move forward, nothing would stop him. His was a deliberative process that was, in part, borne out in his meetings with Massie.

I experienced this myself in briefing Reagan. Once I finally related his disposition in White House briefings to his experience making films—that is, being directed to perform a film role—I could see why Reagan listened so carefully, intently, and was so focused. As an actor, he keyed in on the director, and then when the camera was rolling he jumped into his part and performed. After learning the script and following the director, Reagan made the character come to life. He used this technique in his role as President; however, as the leader of the free world, he was actually portraying himself, and his character was based on his own personal values and beliefs, and it worked—he came across as strong and in command. He put his trust in people who worked for him, and he was most always attentive to their direction. To me, this was a useful lesson in effective leadership. It requires not mindlessness but acute mindfulness, attentiveness, and confidence in the team directing you.

Reagan had both feet planted solidly on the ground, and yet at the same time he was metaphysically processing the dangers occurring on his watch. This caused him to view history and his place in it, as well as the historical events going on around him, in the context of a longer continuum and bigger picture. His unshakable beliefs, optimism, and dedication to service were contributors to how he processed world events. He had, however, both the requirements of his very public career to safeguard and the personal good judgment to keep the full range of his belief systems and faith almost entirely to himself. If he had publicly exposed more about his fundamental principles, or had an unbridled need to share more of his internal thought process, he would have never succeeded in Hollywood or reached the level of leadership he did on an international stage. He kept his personal faith life quiet. This decision ultimately accrued to his benefit.

Patti Davis remembered her father in an interview with *Time* magazine as "a man whose compassion for other people is deep and earnest, and whose spiritual life is based on faith in a loving God, not a vengeful one." She later referred to herself as "the little girl who talked to God about everything because that is what my father did." If Reagan had opened up publicly about the scope and nature of this spiritual dimension in his life, it could have been disastrous to his film and corporate careers, and it also could have been fatal to his political prospects. Hollywood was the perfect warm-up to running for political office, not only because it trained him to be effective in front of cameras but because it exposed him to a community in which, to be a success, you kept many of your personal opinions and beliefs almost completely out of sight—a discipline many politicians do not possess.

This is not to suggest that, though he usually kept his own counsel and measured his words, Reagan was not vocal in Hollywood. In fact, he did pay a price for his outspoken views about communism that resulted, at least once, in a serious threat to his own personal safety and even his ability to continue an acting career. At one time he was threatened with having disfiguring acid thrown on his face, and as a result he started carrying a handgun for his own personal safety. He also experienced this kind of backlash during his days as Governor, when he was challenged by angry mobs of students during the shutdown of the California State University System over budget cuts. This was ideal preparation for the opposition that would, at times, rage against him from opponents during his presidency.

Reagan expressed strong views in strong terms, but he did not engage in the merely emotional barrage of protests sometimes aimed at him. He would rarely be drawn into the contest personally, only in his role as an officeholder. This was typical of his handling of any form of strife or controversy. He was strong and confident but did not typically initiate or react to fiery exchanges. He let his lieutenants handle the skirmishes.

For example, decades later he would handle Gorbachev the same way when, rather than engage the Soviet leader in a prolonged or an angry fight, Reagan simply walked out of their second bilateral summit meeting at Reykjavik, Iceland. He did so over the Soviet leader's persistent demand that Reagan give up his commitment to his signature Strategic Defense Initiative. In its immediate aftermath, the summit was declared a disaster for both men and a lost opportunity for improving bilateral relations.

It wasn't long, however, before it was seen as a decisive win for Reagan. His walking out was calculated on his part, and it drew a definitive line beyond which he would not compromise. After two more summit meetings between the two leaders, the bilateral relationship between the U.S. and the USSR made significant progress, and the Soviet Union itself ultimately disintegrated. The Reykjavik summit, and how Reagan handled it, was a contributing factor. Reagan would not deviate from his principles even in the face of pressure to abandon SDI from many of his own advisors, from a whole host of ridiculers who even used SDI in comedy skits, and from those who wrote about SDI in plentiful editorials.

Reagan held many of his personal views close to his vest, and while it was a wise decision not to indiscriminately disclose these deeply held beliefs, he also paid a price by being misunderstood. This caution inhibited his progress on some issues. His political adversaries and even those who were not decided enemies had him labeled or defined as a person far from who he actually was.

For example, the Russian people for many years held a terrifying, trigger-happy, warmongering image of Reagan, because that was the only image their official news outlets would present—and it was a politically convenient image for them to promote. In fact, at times their streets carried colorful banners of Reagan depicting him as a warmonger and spreading anxiety through its citizenry. They were surprised later when they discovered the man they feared all that time was not fearsome at all. Even many Americans considered Reagan cold, indifferent to the plight of the disadvantaged, remote from those in need, and more attuned to the rich. This may have been a partisan contrivance, but it was not an accurate portrayal.

While he was not the only person in politics or in a leadership role who has carried a significant bearing of faith, Reagan was able to maintain a primarily spiritual disposition without exposing it in a way that would have opened him to ridicule. Some politicians who have, perhaps innocently or from religious fervor, exposed their faith too effusively have been isolated from the opportunities they might otherwise have been accorded in the political realm. Reagan did not generally allow his private faith and beliefs to be associated with political causes or to be used for political purposes, although he was unequivocal about his stance on conservative social issues.

Reagan, though, could not be completely pigeonholed into the tinderbox where politics and faith can be a potentially lethal combination. Without question, however, his faith remained the most significant factor in the decisions he made and the actions he took. He said that in his own words. His faith was the bedrock of his character, and it cannot be discounted in assessing his political impact as a world leader.

Reagan often let those who represented his views—mostly historic leaders, thinkers, and writers the world had come to largely respect—speak for him. To this mix he added his pastors from the Presbyterian Church and a small select group of others he sent on special missions to carry his message. This was an ingenious approach. He put forward an agenda for the American people and then defended it mostly with the words of widely respected leaders and thinkers the world had largely accepted, and who were mostly notable individuals of earlier eras. This was a parallel strategy to the one in which he introduced and honored contemporary heroes at the annual State of the Union address before Congress and the American people via television. These heroes, their lives and actions, illustrated the points Reagan was attempting to make in this annual peroration in a more memorable and sometimes emotional way, and rather than drawing attention away from himself he actually gained praise and personal strength from it.

Reagan's mixture of Biblical quotations with secular ones was famously in evidence in his references to the image of America as a "shining city on a hill." The origin of the quote is Scriptural. In the Gospel of Matthew, Christ tells his followers in the Sermon on the Mount, "You are the light of the world. A city that is set on a hill cannot be hidden." Sixteen hundred years later, John Winthrop, the future Governor of Massachusetts, said to his fellow Pilgrims on landing in the New World, in secular words that echoed the Gospel, "We must consider that we shall be as a city upon a hill." Reagan was not alone in his admiration for Winthrop's inspiring reference. Other Presidents, such as Adams, Lincoln, Kennedy, and Clinton, have invoked the "city on a hill" metaphor as well. Reagan often blended Biblical allusions and secular concepts in this context, such as when he said,

"The lamp of individual conscience burns bright. By that I know we will all be guided to that dreamed-of day when no one wields a sword and no one drags a chain."

In another speech, this one at a Conservative Political Action Committee dinner in 1982, Reagan again combined religious and secular imagery when he said,

"Fellow Americans, our duty is before us tonight. Let us go forward, determined to serve selflessly a vision of man with God, government for the people, and humanity at peace. For it is now our task to tend and preserve, through the darkest and coldest nights, that 'sacred fire of liberty' that President Washington spoke of two centuries ago, a fire that tonight remains a beacon to all the oppressed of the world, shining forth from this kindly, pleasant, greening land we call America."

Reagan, the Preacher in a Global Pulpit

Another important and unusual feature of Reagan as a global leader was that he had an impersonal disposition toward events and people. This was especially useful in bilateral and multilateral negotiations, where he sat at the table across from people with big personalities and large egos. His personal ego was not in the fight . . . just his set of principles. In fact, it would be hard to find a personal ego in Ronald Reagan at all. This is another crucially important concept to grasp about Reagan's character and how it affected his relationships with many world leaders.

What I learned firsthand was that his impersonality or complete lack of personal ego or sensitivity was one of his greatest and yet most subtle strengths as a leader in public life. It was also one of his genuine weaknesses in his private and family life. It was exemplified by that hand-tooled, gold-embossed burgundy leather plaque that was hard for anyone who came into the Oval Office to miss, from cleaning people to heads of state. It sat front and center on his massive historic desk—"There is no limit to what a man can do or where he can go, if he does not mind who gets the credit." This lack of need for approval, acceptance, recognition, acclaim, or fame was one of the rare human qualities and secret ingredients in the impervious armor he wore, armor that was called his Teflon coating by the media. Untoward events and blame did not stick to him, because they did not generally offend him.

Before observing this quality firsthand in Reagan, I would have thought just the opposite was a true characteristic of great leadership—that people who are especially personable and personally sensitive would make the best leaders. Reagan showed me a different way. Being impersonal allowed him to make tough choices based on the principle of the situation rather than having the decision-making process clouded by personal consideration or attachment to people or sentimentality. Margaret Thatcher had this quality as well, and that was why she was called "The Iron Lady."

I remember being in China with him on a state visit when he found out that he owed me some money—a very modest amount. I had taken his wife on a shopping trip for a set of pearls, something many tourists do. I had paid for the pearls, since Presidents and their wives don't usually carry much money, if any. When he found out about it, he wanted to remedy that right away. I told him we had much more important things to focus on, much more important work to do. He wouldn't hear of it. He insisted on our walking into his bedroom in the lavish State Guest House in Beijing, where he took out his personal checkbook. Still I protested that he shouldn't be bothered with it at the time. "What was the exact dollar amount again?" he quizzed, and he quickly wrote out a check to repay the debt. (The ironic thing, of course, about checks from Presidents is that you never really want to cash them because of their possible future historic value!)

When we returned to Washington, he called me at home one night and asked me if I could find a bracelet for Nancy to match the necklace she had bought in Beijing. Even in an exchange as mundane and personal as that, he would treat you as if you were his best friend—and yet there was an undertone of impersonality or slight detachment about it that was difficult to describe. This quality, though subtle, was also felt and observed by many others, and it was apparently with him throughout his life. I believe it gave him his ability to deflect criticism, stay focused, and be a strong leader without complicating his own personality.

Auditioning for President While Riding the Rails for GE

Reagan's years working as spokesman for General Electric (GE) are especially important to consider in relation to his later role as a global leader and communicator. It was during those years that he was researching major public policy issues from different perspectives in order to build his own platform of political positions and ideas. He wrote all of his own speeches in longhand on yellow legal pads (a preference of his during the presidency as well), crafting and editing a message he could adopt as his own.

During this time, from 1954 to 1962, when he rode the train for GE because of his fear of flying, the speaker and his speeches were becoming synchronized. He always professed and confirmed his individual beliefs and values when discussing company and more general issues with factory workers and management alike. During this time he completed his migration from Democrat to Republican. He insisted on writing his own speeches and would not merely mouth the corporate policy that was handed to him. This practice allowed him to develop his independent views, and in his delivery of them he integrated his views with the message. This work was perhaps even more valuable to his preparation for the presidency than the staging and script reading that he did to prepare for the fifty-three motion pictures in which he performed.

The hundreds of handwritten GE speeches, discovered by Martin and Annalise Anderson, two acclaimed professors at Stanford University who had served Reagan in California and Washington, provide concrete evidence of Reagan's thought processes and his personal writing ability. In his GE job he had no bank of ingenious speechwriters assigned to him, as he later did in the White House. In these handwritten speeches there was also evidence of actual research into facets and facts of the various issues he wanted to address in his GE talks.

A preview of the presidential brand he developed and honed during his GE days was debuted, to unexpected success, in a nationally televised and now iconic speech. He was selected to introduce Barry Goldwater, an old friend of Nancy Reagan's family and candidate for President, at the 1964 Republican National Convention in Phoenix. The result was that Reagan, the conservative Republican, was officially launched into the national public arena. His political career was unexpectedly inaugurated at this convention. The content of his widely noticed speech formed the core of his own personal platform, which had been developed during his days on the road for GE. This speech was called "A Time for Choosing."

In his book, *The Education of Ronald Reagan: The General Electric Years and the Untold Story of His Conversion to Conservatism*, Thomas W. Evans writes about the GE period in Reagan's career this way: "Ronald Reagan developed a vision of America during his GE years. He learned to reduce his views to a few simple precepts...His methods of absorbing massive amounts of material, of writing and delivering his speeches, were unique. Perhaps the most persuasive statements confirming his education during his General Electric years come from the Reagans themselves. In her autobiography, Nancy Reagan wrote that 'if you believe, as Ronnie does, that everything happens for a purpose, then certainly there was a hidden purpose in Ronnie's job with General Electric.'"

Reagan himself referred to his GE years as his *"post-graduate education in political science"* and observed that *"it wasn't a bad apprenticeship for someone who'd someday enter public life."* He spoke of his *"self-conversion"* during these years, and that he ended up *"preaching sermons"* about his strongly held beliefs. His speechwriters at the White House admitted using the speeches of the GE years as the basis of some of their own drafts. During the General Electric days when he was thinking, researching, writing, and speaking, Reagan learned how to do what he would do as President—turn his beliefs, vision, and character into significant electoral victories and steer the course of history through persuasive leading and talking.

In the Reagan GE speeches his emerging ideology became clearer. In Schenectady, New York, in 1959 (as related to me by a nonagenarian friend of mine who was there), he said, *"We have been told by economists down through the years that if the total tax burden ever reaches 25 percent, we are in danger of undermining our private enterprise system."* He continued to build his repertoire, and in 1961, he added what was perhaps obvious to many, although often left unsaid by politicians, that *"the ideological struggle with Russia is the number one problem in the world."* By 1964, when drafting the Goldwater address, he borrowed from and built on his GE speeches when he said famously:

"I'd like to suggest there is no such thing as a left or right. There's only an up or down. Up to the maximum of individual freedom consistent with law and order, or down to the ant heap of totalitarianism... You and I have a rendezvous with destiny. We'll preserve for our children this, the last best hope of man on earth, or we'll sentence them to take the last step into a thousand years of darkness. If we fail, at least our children and our children's children, will say of us, we justified our brief moment here. We did all that could be done."

In this part of the speech he was publicly announcing his lifelong attachment to a metaphoric allusion to light and darkness.

At GE he could try out more conservative views and actually make the full transition from registered Democrat to Republican, a metamorphosis that was complete by the time of the Goldwater convention and the "Time for Choosing" speech in 1964. It was on those long trips—crisscrossing the country by train, visiting 139 GE plants in forty states, and speaking to more than 250,000 people at the factory gates— that he previewed viewpoints on public issues that he later put to use in official public service. The GE years actually readied him for national politics and gave him a platform—although at that time he could not have known what might lie ahead for him. GE offered him a fully financed (to the tune of a $125,000-per-year salary) period of message development and the time to carve his principles and beliefs in stone.

With the sponsorship of GE, he was getting good results in improved labor relations and goodwill for the company. Reagan had steady crowds at these speaking engagements, and during a period when he was away from home for weeks at a time, he wrote to Nancy that the crowds seemed genuinely interested in what he had to say. GE was increasingly proud of Reagan, and for his part he felt that he was really earning his yearly salary—which was an impressive sum at that time. But he was earning something else far more valuable to his future and ultimately for the world than his fee. The responses he got from the crowds on the GE trips provided him with invaluable feedback that resulted in constant refinements and edits to his presentations. Reagan would rework his speeches on the train and then try out a new line, story, or quote at the next stop.

Lem Boulware, a GE Vice President and the man who worked most closely with Reagan, wrote, "It's the job of... every citizen—to go back to school in economics, individually in small groups and in big groups... to learn from simple textbooks, from organized courses, from individual discussions with business associates, in neighborhood groups... This was a summary of the process that became the education of Ronald Reagan, and as Reagan became increasingly a participant, this was the beginning of his role in the conservative revolution in America."

Most anyone who worked for Reagan would say that once he reached the White House his beliefs were so strongly entrenched that he was mostly unmovable and stubborn when challenged on them. It was during these earlier career deployments, however, that he was changing, honing, refining, and improving various messages and approaches. This was a time for creating the principles he ultimately lived by, rules that he put into practice in public life during his two terms as Governor of California from 1968 to 1976 and then in his final job as President.

There is another possible cause for this obstinacy—a trait in evidence in his White House years but often overlooked. It was simply that he entered the ultimate spotlight when he was older than any other man who had gained the highest office. Reagan was sixty-nine when elected, and he served from the age of seventy almost to his seventy-eighth birthday. By comparison, George Washington (who, frozen in time, we think of as eternally old) was only fifty-seven when inaugurated, and John F. Kennedy was forty-three. Theodore Roosevelt was the youngest to assume the office of chief executive at forty-two. The President closest in age to Reagan was my own ancestor William Henry Harrison; elected at age sixty-eight, he was dead from pneumonia or sepsis within weeks of his inauguration!

Reagan frequently and famously joked about his age and used it to his advantage in self-deprecating ways. I think his age gave him a more mature and experienced point of view—or playbook—if for no other reason than because he had simply been at work longer and had more on-the-job experience than some other political leaders. He had been in front of the camera and in public speaking for more years than his competitors. This was a numerical leg up. He was not, at that stage of his life, about to give up the principles he had worked so hard for and had come to depend upon. Reagan had been an understudy for the role of a lifetime for much longer than most. Even his failed bid for the Republican nomination in 1976 gave him more seasoning and maturity, not to mention a better experienced team that helped put him over the finish line in his final win in 1980. In looking back, I did not really consider the Reagans' age at all when either scheduling them or traveling with them. For me they were young and capable of anything—and yet this could not have been true. I remember going in back doors and up staircases with them. Out of sight of the public they preferred taking the steps two or three at a time and bounding up as fast as they could to keep in shape. We staff members and the Secret Service had to keep up. While the President was not a jogger or tennis player—preferring horseback riding, building fences, and chopping wood for outdoor exercise—I clearly remember his daily commitment to working out in the private gym that was installed in one of the two front bedrooms in the family quarters. He told me with pride that he had added muscle tone following the assassination attempt. His gym routine was a daily ritual that I often observed.

Reagan's obstinate streak provided consternation to some on the White House staff, Cabinet officials, and bureaucrats who would, at times, ply him with plentiful reasons why he should moderate or alter his views or official position on one issue or another. Some officials rejected portions of his speech drafts and provided him with policy options that reflected more of their own views than his. I observed senior advisors, and even his wife, devise unique ways to reach Reagan with compelling arguments they wanted him to consider and even adopt. I also observed them trying circuitously to influence him or to convince him to change a strongly held position by going around him, avoiding direct confrontation—which they knew he would not like.

This was why the unique triumvirate of James Baker, Ed Meese, and Mike Deaver, as his most senior aides, was essential to protecting Reagan and to allowing him to be himself. Deaver and Nancy Reagan conferred every morning on the President's disposition and his attitudes about various issues. They formed a close-knit team to sometimes urge him to change or moderate positions in ways they considered important to his legacy. This interplay between staff and the President's spouse to influence his rock-solid views and opinions was a prominent part of the daily dynamics of the Reagan White House.

At times White House observers felt that Reagan was dominated by Nancy and that she was the real power in this political couple. Furthermore his opponents used Nancy Reagan's perceived position of power to denigrate Reagan or to reduce his own power, replacing it with some of hers. From my vantage point of working for both of them, I could see that she was a hardworking, smart, fiercely loyal, and supportive spouse, yet I could also see that Reagan rarely yielded his position on policy issues to the First Lady. Reagan himself was not about to be controlled by anyone. She frequently stated the obvious that she alone had the last word at night and the first word in the morning with the President. There is no question that she influenced and may have moderated his position on certain issues, but he held tightly to the reins. In this way he was the decidedly dominant force between the two of them when it came to his work.

While Reagan did modify his views on some critical issues, or at least his manner in communicating about these issues, he always reserved judgment about what he thought was right. He was a staunch defender of people who worked for him, perhaps even unwisely—people such as David Stockman, his budget director, who ridiculed Reagan's supply-side economic programs, and Labor Secretary Ray Donovan, who fell under criminal investigation for alleged illegal activities in the New York construction industry but was later exonerated. It was hard for him to actually believe a person could be ill intentioned—even though he had surely seen many unscrupulous people in his lifetime.

Reagan was wary of some bureaucratic policy makers, government officials, and others who offered their advice and tried to navigate his course for him from their own wheelhouse. He may have been naïve about some who sought to take advantage of him to build their own credibility. Nancy Reagan sought to shore up what she thought was her husband's vulnerability on personnel issues by weighing in on Administration appointments, including ambassadorial posts and the firing of his second Chief of Staff, Don Regan.

Because Reagan was conflict averse and avoided head-on collisions with those who wronged him or those who needed to be disciplined, he rarely confronted the very people who might have plainly benefited from it. It took mounting pressure on Reagan from many quarters to move him to fire Regan, just as it had been difficult to fire Al Haig, his first Secretary of State. As journalist and biographer Lou Cannon wrote, Reagan's "stubborn streak did not yield easily to the demands of staff or spouse," especially "when a member of the Reagan team was under fire on a question of judgment or ethics from a White House official, the Democrats, the media, or a combination of the three."

Reagan did not generally see or label people as bad, evil, or dishonest. He tended to just see the good in people—not some fantasy goodness—in a way that was practical and useful for him. I think he had spent so many years looking on the bright side of things that it was almost impossible for him to imagine a human being as malicious. That does not mean that he did not see and strenuously call out impersonal or political evil for what it was; however, he did not view evil as personal or see people as inherently or individually evil.

I sat with him a few times watching the evening news, up in the family quarters, which invariably included something about Reagan that was completely false and at least irritating. Yes, he could get angry in these circumstances, but I did not have the feeling he was blaming a particular reporter or that he was spiteful or hateful. What some might call passivity was actually a very practical tool of effective leadership, especially in negotiating with individuals who might not have been personally very likeable or who held unfavorable attitudes toward the United States.

As a result, France's socialist President François Mitterrand, China's Deng Xiaoping, and Soviet leader Mikhail Gorbachev, though they had serious political disagreements with Reagan, stated that they were drawn to him on a personal level. This was apparent to many of us, and, according to Lou Cannon, an official who attended meetings Reagan had with heads of state said, "Reagan the man, the politician, fascinated them. It was almost as if they were saying, 'What does this man have that works so well for him?' It was like they wanted to bottle it, take it home, and use it themselves."

Reagan's well-known rock-solid stance on issues also helped make him understandable to the public on a world platform. This was ironic, since for several years in the run-up to the election, he was characterized by his opponents as trigger-happy, shallow, unreliable, and changeable—to list words often used by journalists to describe him. In actuality, Reagan turned out to be one of the most stable and steady Presidents. The public always knew where he stood on an issue, because he repeated his position for them over and over again. During his eight years, the public was mostly focused on jobs, economic growth and security, taxes, and eliminating the threat of conflict with another superpower, the Soviet Union. These were obvious, though complex, issues for Reagan and his time. Within this economic and foreign policy climate, Reagan set the agenda and drove it for most of his eight years. That was the point of the "Theme for the Day" task force on which I served for a time—putting Reagan squarely in control of the agenda. The U.S. presidency held a heightened and uniquely powerful position in the world during those eight years, and he felt obligated to keep it there and use the power and the prestige he garnered to America's advantage.

This *known quantity* aspect of Reagan, as well as his strength as a leader, was a plus in bilateral relationships with other heads of state and with the U.S. Congress as well. It must have been relatively easy for foreign leaders to prepare for meetings with Reagan, because his positions radiated out from his personal beliefs and were well publicized and documented. The dynamic situations in various regions of the world were sometimes more complex than his basic beliefs could address; however, they were the bedrock from which he developed more detailed and specific policy positions on issues as they arose. An example might be his response to Thatcher's 1982 invasion of the Falkland Islands off the coast of Argentina. Thatcher sought and expected Reagan's endorsement of her adventure, and she was surprised to find Reagan unwilling to condone her decision.

Reagan's Belief in America and Its Relationship with the Rest of the World

A central plank in Reagan's foundational beliefs was the concept of American Exceptionalism. This did not mean, for him, that Americans were superior to people of other nations. It did mean that the *ideals* on which America was founded were absolutely superior and necessary for the promotion and protection of democracy throughout the world. This belief embraced the view that ultimately the U.S. government, as the most effective form of democracy the world has experienced, had the responsibility to help create free and open societies, promote and protect individual liberties, and help engineer a path to economic growth and stability for all peoples. He also believed that in so doing America also protected its own way of life against threats from foreign and unfriendly sources. This was the essential light Reagan was referring to when he spoke about the "shining city on a hill." Reagan truly felt that if the light from these ideals were to extinguish or even to dim, the rest of the world could suffer.

Reagan remained unmovable in his belief that building

up and maintaining a strong military while he conducted an assertive verbal indictment of the evils of communism would have its intended effect. While he played his role, the State Department and the Pentagon deployed specific and comprehensive diplomatic and military strategies and initiatives as part of his strategy. Nancy Reagan herself sought to soften the President's rhetoric and encouraged an easing in his tone in ways she felt could contribute to a lasting thaw in U.S.-Soviet relations. While he was not unmindful of her entreaties, often made through third parties, he never abdicated what he saw as his principal responsibility to do the job in the way that would accomplish the greatest good—despite what others, including Nancy, thought he should do. He heard what those around him were suggesting, but he had his own plan and he would not be deterred in carrying it out. He was an independent man. He was a loner; he was willing to go alone on issues and language about which he felt strongly.

One example of Reagan's singular focus—and also his foresight—was his proposal for a space-based missile shield to defend the United States. Reagan called it the Strategic Defense Initiative (SDI). His critics called it Star Wars. Those critics also called it reckless, unrealistic, too expensive, and a recipe for starting a nuclear war. But Reagan, as usual, stood by his vision, defied his critics, and used SDI as a key element in his arsenal to help bring down the Soviet Union. When Reagan refused to give up SDI at the 1987 Reykjavik, Iceland, summit with Gorbachev, his Soviet counterparts knew their country would never win the Cold War as long as Reagan was in charge. "Looking back," Margaret Thatcher later wrote, "it is now clear to me that Ronald Reagan's original decision on SDI was the single most important of his presidency." She said that his "refusal to trade away SDI...was crucial to the victory over communism." SDI was a specific tactic to fulfill a strategy of peace through strength.

In his presidential role, where clever storytelling could be useful, Reagan charmed many heads of state. This even included General Secretary Gorbachev, who described Reagan as a master storyteller, and who especially enjoyed Reagan's tales of Hollywood. According to the author Frances FitzGerald, Gorbachev and his wife, Raisa, "devoured the details" of Reagan's Hollywood days, "his career in the movies, how movies were produced, how different directors worked, [and] how various stars behaved in real life." They "seemed pleased to be in the company of someone who had known Jimmy Stewart, John Wayne, and Humphrey Bogart."

I know from my own experience that Gorbachev told the President he had watched old Reagan movies in preparation for their first meeting in Geneva. I found it hard to believe, though, that Raisa had that much interest, as I always found her lecturing or scolding Nancy Reagan about the value of the collective, communist way of life. She was, however, fascinated with the West, and she used her American Express card freely when visiting London and other Western cities; and yet she stayed true to her academic training as a college professor at Moscow University focused on the history and values of socialism.

Brian Mulroney, Prime Minister of Canada, and also a great storyteller himself, told me that Reagan came to life for him "in his stories, and they were always put to good use in our G5 meetings and elsewhere." To him, Reagan was the master at using illustrations "to lead and to teach—without placing himself in the direct line of fire." Margaret Thatcher, who was also on the receiving end of many Reagan stories, appeared to take them all in good humor. At his eighty-third birthday party in 1994, she admitted the importance of his storytelling. She said, "With that Irish twinkle and that easy homespun style, which never changed, you brought a new assurance to America...It was not only that you were the Great Communicator—and you were the greatest—but that you had a message to communicate. The message that had inspired the Founding Fathers, the message that has guided this nation from its birth—the essence of good government is to blend the wisdom of the ages with the circumstances of contemporary times—that is what you did. Not since Lincoln or Winston Churchill in Britain has there been a President who has so understood the power of words to uplift and to inspire." Then Thatcher added, most strikingly, "Like Winston Churchill, you made words fight like soldiers and lifted the spirit of a nation."

CHAPTER FIVE

Words That Fight like Soldiers

As Reagan's motorcade came to a halt in front of Berlin's historic Brandenburg Gate on June 12, 1987, he told the staffers in the traveling party with him, just as he alighted from his car to give a speech, *"The boys at the State Department are not going to like this."*

He was under the surveillance of armed guards standing watch atop their security posts a hundred yards away in East Berlin; their binoculars were trained on the American President for the duration of his brief stop there. Reagan was about to speak the six most remembered words of his presidency and perhaps among the most famous of the last century. Six words that eventually echoed around the world. Six words that fought like soldiers.

"Mr. Gorbachev, tear down this wall."

These six words had an impact intended and expected by Reagan but never imagined by many of the wise men and women of his own Administration. They were almost not spoken at all and had been intentionally deleted several times from his formal speech text by U.S. government officials. George Shultz, then Secretary of State, doubted that the words would meet their intended purpose. Shortly before the speech he said, "I really think the line about tearing down the Wall is going to be an affront to Mr. Gorbachev." And Gorbachev, seen as the intended target of Reagan's words (actually the Soviet system was the target), stated later that "this did not really impress us as it did you. We knew very well that the profession of President Reagan was an actor, a performer. So he did a performance. But nevertheless, this did not diminish—did not diminish the role and the importance of these processes of President Reagan."

Reagan understood the power of words carefully chosen and delivered to dramatic effect at the right time; however, unlike the soundstages of Hollywood, this was a world stage, and the stakes were not just movie reviews but major shifts in world power.

The power of these memorable words was building far in advance of the delivery of the speech and not in isolation from related initiatives at the State Department and Pentagon. Before Reagan called on Mr. Gorbachev to "tear down this wall," he was carefully building up a structure to support greater mutual understanding between the two men, so that when these words were spoken, they were heard and understood in the correct context by Gorbachev and by the Russian and German people. These words had to carry with them an authority and certainty that could not be denied or mocked. Because of Reagan's skill in delivering and timing this message, and because of his confidence that Gorbachev could and should tear it down for the good of the German people and the whole world, Gorbachev knew what Reagan meant, and it gave him an opening as well. It was as if Reagan were the quarterback passing the ball to his Soviet counterpart in the fourth quarter.

He knew how serious Reagan was and that he was a man who would not compromise his position nor relinquish his goal to stop the spread of communism.

Had Reagan made that call prior to his previous bilateral face-to-face meetings with Gorbachev, it could have provoked a different response that might have blocked the burgeoning and productive relationship they had. Timing was everything. At this point, Gorbachev knew Reagan as a strong and determined yet reasonable human being who believed in God as Gorbachev also did—to a certain extent. Gorbachev accepted Reagan's mental muscularity and verbal acuity. In addition to that, he was reacting from the perspective of his own plans for the future of the USSR. He was a determined and forceful leader in his own right. He didn't need Reagan to tell him what to do, but he may have used Reagan as a cover for what he *did* do in various stages following this speech.

The 1987 Brandenburg Gate speech also illustrated the complexity of negotiations often practiced by Reagan and his Administration. While Reagan's speeches took the high and lofty road of pragmatic idealism, there were always intense ongoing negotiations under way on diplomatic and military levels. In this case, the speech was delivered against a backdrop of serious debates in Germany over the strategic placement of NATO intermediate-range nuclear missiles in response to the deployment of new Soviet SS-20 warheads.

A great deal of this controversy was being managed by Richard Burt, the very capable U.S. Ambassador to Germany who was stationed in Bonn, and his colleague in Berlin, John Kornblum. Along with their other colleagues, they determined that a visit and a high-minded powerful speech by Reagan was just what was needed at the time. They worked with the

White House advance team to scour the city for appropriate venues, and were repeatedly rebuffed by West Berlin officials over their decision to take Reagan to that powerful site overlooking the East and the Bundestag, the former seat of the unified German government, which was located near the iconic Brandenburg Gate. They had to deal with repeated attempts by the Germans to change the venue for this speech. Nonetheless, the White House advance office and Kornblum fought for and won their decision about that specific location, with its searing and graphic backdrop of a divided city.

There were those at the State Department, the National Security Council, and the White House—including Reagan's own Chief of Staff, Howard Baker—who were fundamentally opposed to the inclusion of those memorable words in his speech and argued for their removal. But they were overruled by Reagan himself, and his imperative about the Wall ultimately stayed in the speech. Reagan knew that he had already built a relationship of mutual understanding, if not complete agreement, with Gorbachev, and that was why his words were spoken with courage and confidence. These are "soldier" words that ultimately brought results.

"Tear down this wall!" Reagan knew he was also speaking to the broader world and to "walls" that needed to be torn down in other parts of the globe as well. These words were not just for Berlin that day, where Reagan had gone to celebrate the city's 750th birthday. They were about any walls that keep people from self-determination and freedom, and any walls that deprive people of the freedom to worship God in their own way, as Reagan stated clearly in the concluding section of the speech.

Reagan knew the value of deep and sustained confidence

in bold ideas that could figuratively move mountains, and he had the authority and the courage to mold them into a verbal demand as well as the strength of character to convey them. That was why it worked. This is not to say that mere words alone brought down the Berlin Wall; however, they did help to sway and support the public will to do so. These flint-like words provided a spark. Keeping these memorable words in the speech also represented a victory over those policy makers who held a limited view of what the United States should be doing or could actually achieve in foreign policy anywhere in the world. It was a clash between those who believed that the United States had an intrinsic calling, embedded in the founding, to actively bring freedom to all peoples and those who did not.

The inspiration for these words came from a trip that Peter Robinson, a hardworking and brilliant Reagan speechwriter, took to Germany prior to drafting the speech. Peter told me that on his preadvance trip to Berlin, he met with a small group of West German people who suggested to him that Reagan should call on Gorbachev to get rid of the Wall and that the timing was right for it. That idea captivated Peter, and he brought this proposal back to the staff speechwriting meeting with the President in the Oval Office. After it was written and the draft was circulated among various staff reviewers, a strong lobbying effort erupted against its inclusion from almost all quarters. Ultimately, and in the few minutes prior to his arrival at the Brandenburg Gate, as his motorcade pulled up, Reagan himself decided to include it. He probably knew all along that would be the case.

That day at the Brandenburg Gate and for the entire world to hear, Reagan said, in part,

"We welcome change and openness; for we believe that freedom and security go together, that the advance of human liberty can only strengthen the cause of world peace. There is one sign the Soviets can make that would be unmistakable, that would advance dramatically the cause of freedom and peace. General Secretary Gorbachev, if you seek peace, if you seek prosperity for the Soviet Union and Eastern Europe, if you seek liberalization, come here to this gate. Mr. Gorbachev, open this gate! Mr. Gorbachev, tear down this wall!"

Later in his speech, President Reagan said,

"As I looked out a moment ago from the Reichstag, that embodiment of German unity, I noticed words crudely spray-painted upon the wall, perhaps by a young Berliner, 'This wall will fall. Beliefs become reality.' Yes, across Europe, this wall will fall. For it cannot withstand faith; it cannot withstand truth. The wall cannot withstand freedom."

Here was Reagan, the strategist, harkening back, as he did so often, to faith, freedom, and truth. And then there was evil. Reagan had called out the Soviet Union as an evil empire in an earlier speech on March 3, 1983. This term turned the foreign policy world and the media upside down. It was well documented, however, that at least four previous Presidents had described communist regimes in precisely the same or even more severe terms. It was this speech that built the pedestal on which Reagan could later stand in Berlin and make the demand he did some years later. Here was how the "Evil Empire" speech paved the way:

"Yes, let us pray for the salvation of all of those who live in that totalitarian darkness—pray they will discover the joy of knowing God. But until they do, let us be aware that while they preach the supremacy of the state, declare its omnipotence over individual man, and predict its eventual domination of all peoples on the earth, they are the focus of evil in the modern world.

"It was C. S. Lewis who, in his unforgettable Screwtape Letters, *wrote: 'The greatest evil is not done now in those sordid "dens of crime" that Dickens loved to paint. It is not even done in concentration camps and labor camps. In those we see its final result. But it is conceived and ordered . . . in clear, carpeted, warmed, and well-lighted offices by quiet men with white collars and cut fingernails and smooth-shaven cheeks who do not need to raise their voices.'*

"Well, because these 'quiet men' do not 'raise their voices,' because they sometimes speak in soothing tones of brotherhood and peace, because, like other dictators before them, they're always making 'their final territorial demand,' some would have us accept them at their word and accommodate ourselves to their aggressive impulses. But if history teaches anything, it teaches that simple-minded appeasement or wishful thinking about our adversaries is folly. It means the betrayal of our past, the squandering of our freedom.

"So, I urge you to speak out against those who would place the United States in a position of military and moral inferiority. You know, I've always believed that old Screwtape reserved his best efforts for those of you in the church. So, in your discussions of the nuclear freeze proposals, I urge you to beware the temptation of pride—the temptation of blithely declaring yourselves above it all and label both sides equally at fault, to ignore the facts of history and the aggressive impulses of an evil empire, to simply call the arms race a giant misunderstanding and thereby remove yourself from the struggle between right and wrong and good and evil."

Reagan might have been a sunny optimist, but he was also acquainted with evil, and he had the raw courage to call it out where he saw it. He knew that identifying evil where he saw it was the first step in destroying it. He cared about mankind that much—and cared that little about what others would think of him for saying it. Reagan also knew that to really comprehend and benefit from the power of good required an understanding of evil. It was his view that this enlightened position would better frame the debate about the most appropriate and deadening response to tyranny. To frame and isolate evil was a critical note in the Reagan symphonic approach to bringing down communism, and it was critical to the whole operation and its success. This showed Reagan as a thinker who had the capacity to see the geopolitical picture as it was evolving and to discern and fulfill his role in it.

Reagan's communication strategy and its deployment was like a puzzle. Every piece was needed to make it work. To reveal the whole picture. The principles had to be in place; the communicating skills had to be present; the opportunities and venues for delivering the message had to be devised; and the moral life and authenticity of the communicator had to fit the job that needed to be done. These elements were all present in Berlin in 1987. The earlier 1983 speech defining the Soviet system as evil had been noted, debated, and recorded and had done its work, and now the demand for action was being made. These two speeches—the Evil Empire speech in 1983 and Berlin Wall speech in 1987—were actually bookends in Reagan's well-timed crusade to rid the world of communism.

In reality Reagan said these six words about the Wall over and over again in so many ways that they were eventually avoided if not ridiculed by most journalists at the time. But not by history. These words—*"Mr. Gorbachev, tear down this wall"*— were repeated until they had their impact with the intended audience. In the West these words were heard more because of the controversy surrounding them, which resembled a dust storm in the media. Reagan must have assumed this would happen, and he must have calculated this and been ready for it.

These memorable six words, inflammatory and demanding as they seemed to be, were not immediately acknowledged for their power and effect for some time following the speech. What was more, it took another two years before the Wall actually came down. It was then that Reagan's words were recalled and, of course, debated as to their possible relationship to what history was witnessing. The credit for the Wall coming down accrued to the courage of many, including Pope John Paul II, Mikhail Gorbachev, and Margaret Thatcher, and the unique timing of history. Most important of all were the masses of people who actually took it down with their own hands. Few would deny that, at minimum, these words constituted the bugle call that led the charge. Words that were publicly uttered with a high degree of risk and led the charge just like a standard-bearer. That is fascinating in itself. Reagan himself, however, would never take credit for the Wall coming down. He said the credit belonged to many people, first and foremost the German people. But also—and more important, in his mind, I think—he felt it was due to divine intervention.

The question of verifiable impact from his speech lingered in my mind. I had a unique opportunity to assess it on my own after the end of Reagan's second term. Shortly after the Wall came down, I was working in Berlin on a large real estate development project at Checkpoint Charlie, which was a former official border crossing at the Wall in the middle of the city. I was also working with the Treuhand, a government agency initiative to sell former East German companies and factories to Western buyers. During this time, I was privileged to meet with Berliners and other Eastern Europeans who had lived under the totalitarian rule and oppression imposed by the Soviet Bloc.

I asked them what they heard that day at the Brandenburg Gate regarding the call to bring the Wall down, and I also asked them what they thought of Reagan's previous labeling of the Soviet regime as evil. What they told me of their views was later verified by independent polling of large samples of East Germans following the collapse of the Soviet Union.

What my German and Eastern European friends told me was that when Reagan called out the regime under which they lived as evil and repeated it over and over again, people who heard it, and who had been reluctant to admit it before, actually began to believe it—to see it more objectively for what it was. This labeling the Soviets as evil and the call to bring down the Wall were like the consistent pounding of the hammer on a rock; sooner or later the recurring force breaks the hard surface. In this case it was the breaking of what was then called the "big lie" theory—the lie imposed on ordinary citizens that communism was the supreme and only legitimate effective form of government, fostering economic stability, prosperity, and freedom. Once there was an opening in the minds of the people toward the possibility of change and an admission that it might be done without retaliatory military action, their desire to be free of oppression provided the energy to accomplish it. The Wall came down as a result—and with it came an essential lesson in history.

In examining how Reagan accomplished what he did in crafting and delivering the Brandenburg Gate speech, it's plain that he used several effective tactics. First, he employed an unexpected and startling command that he knew, or at least suspected, could be fulfilled. He did not call for this action just to be dramatic, goading, or challenging without being purposeful. I believe that Reagan envisioned the Wall coming down and knew that Gorbachev could and would allow it. When Reagan made that statement, he was really giving Gorbachev the political cover he needed to look the other way when, through unplanned circumstances, people started tearing it down.

But simply calling for something to be done if it were knowingly unachievable might have cost Reagan his credibility and could have been soundly dismissed. Reagan had taught me that you should never launch a campaign of any kind unless you are certain you have already won. In this case, if the command had not been grounded in stark and universally accepted reality, and also had not been placed in the context of a larger campaign to end communism, it might have seemed imperious, for the sake of personal or political ambition, and would have rung hollow. The command had to be for some sort of noble or moral purpose—and it surely was. Kennedy made a call on Americans to serve their country and to join him in sending a man to the moon. Churchill commanded his countrymen to rise to the defense of freedom. Heroic calls for action that have staying power and bring about a desired result are rare, but they are also instructive historically and provide a path forward to those who respond.

Next, Reagan's memorable Brandenburg Gate words set forth a plan or vision for the future. Reagan wanted to be able to look back on his words and see what was accomplished as a result of his having spoken them. In Reagan's case, the Berlin Wall did fall, and its falling was a key feature in Germany's future. Reagan's words are forever linked to this future. Of course, not all calls for action achieve results, and some messages without outcomes may also become memorable for other reasons. Dr. Martin Luther King's historic and deeply moving

"I Have a Dream" speech dramatically set forth his vision for the future and a call for action that is still used to measure the mixed accomplishments of the civil rights movement.

Finally, there had been a strategic buildup to Reagan's six memorable words and an undergirding for their sustainability. These words were stated in context of a larger policy objective. They were not spoken in isolation. They were actionable. They required a response. People knew instantly what Reagan meant, even though the words were still challenged by governmental officials on both sides of the Wall.

The Power of Words Deliberately Chosen

Reagan's most successful and inspiring speeches sprang from his desire to recruit others to join him in his effort to seek what he called, when he quoted from the character Ulysses in one of his favorite poems written by Alfred, Lord Tennyson, *"a newer world."* An example of this was the speech he gave in 1985 in the interest of promoting German reunification at an annual youth encampment in the Bavarian Alps.

In an effort to locate the ancient castle where this speech was to take place, we on the presidential advance team found ourselves closer to death than most of us had ever been before—or so I believed. A small group of us, representing the President, were aboard German Chancellor Helmut Kohl's personal helicopter on a preadvance survey trip in the Rhineland-Palatinate state of Germany, scouting various ancient sites and other more modern speech venues. The chopper hit a sudden and violent storm and was flying blind in the clouds, which might be acceptable if you are in a fixed-wing aircraft at thirty-seven thousand feet, but we were hugging evergreen mountains and riding up one side of the strong air pockets and down the other—at treetop level.

While I could not see anything out the windows of the chopper, I could imagine the news headlines: "White House Staff Perishes on Presidential Mission in Bavarian Alps." Our white-knuckle trek lasted for what seemed like an hour but was probably only half of that when the pilot finally saw a clearing and landed. We were shaken but alive.

What we were searching for was worth the threatening flight. We discovered an ancient historic castle where there would be a German youth camp in session during an upcoming state visit to Germany by President Reagan. The President's goal was to talk directly to the people of Germany and this time to the future leaders of that country rather than the current established political or governmental machinery. This was a hallmark of Reagan—to speak directly and openly to groups of ordinary citizens whenever he could, just as much as he spoke to lawmakers and individual heads of state. This was more effective than talking through the sieve of the media. Reagan was at his best when delivering the message directly to constituents and groups of citizens.

Our job on that foggy and stormy day was to decide on this site for a major speech about freedom and unity. We climbed all over the castle, including the craggy walls, and found that it had an almost cinematic quality about it: centuries old, deteriorating, and massive. A perfect backdrop for Reagan. What's more, this castle was also considered the symbol of the democracy movement in nineteenth-century Germany, which is celebrated, especially by young people, in its yearly festival.

When we returned with the President several weeks later,

we felt right at home, because although Marine One, the President's chopper, could now land safely, there was lingering fog—which created a sort of mystical atmosphere for the day. But in the case of the thousands of German youth assembled that morning in the Bavarian Alps, Reagan's call for them to spring to action to defend individual liberty and support a united Europe was anything but foggy. Here is some of what he said in what became one of my personal favorites among the many speeches I had witnessed:

"I am only a visitor to your country, but I am proud to stand with you today by these walls of Schloss Hambach. They are walls of time that cradle the glorious past and that reach toward the promise of a future written for eternity across this wide-open sky. Think back to that first Festival of Freedom that was held here in 1832. What noble vision it was that inspired and emboldened your first patriots—not violence, not destruction of society, and not some far-flung utopian scheme. No, their vision and cry were revolutionary in the truest sense of that word. Those first patriots cried out for a free, democratic, and united Germany, and we do so again today. They cried out for solidarity with freedom fighters in Poland, and we do so again today. And they waved the colors of black, red, and gold to announce rebirth of human spirit and dignity, and those colors wave proudly here today . . .

"Your future awaits you, so take up your responsibilities and embrace your opportunities with enthusiasm and pride in Germany's strength. Understand that there are no limits to how high each of you can climb . . . Let us ask ourselves: What is at the heart of freedom? In the answer lies the deepest hope for the future of mankind and the reason there can be no walls around those who are determined to be free. Each of us, each of you, is made in the most enduring, powerful image of Western civilization. We're made in the image of God, the image of God, the Creator . . .

"The future awaits your creation. From your ranks can come a new Bach, Beethoven, Goethe, and Otto Hahn for Germany's future . . . My young friends, believe me, this is a wonderful time to be alive and to be free. Remember that in your hearts are the stars of your fate; remember that everything depends on you; and remember not to let one moment slip away, for as Schiller has told us, 'He who has done his best for his own time has lived for all times.'"

Standing in the audience, shoulder to shoulder with the packed crowds, I attempted to honestly gauge their reaction. I saw how many of them were visibly moved that day because of the President's words and because of their commitment to and strong desire for a united Germany. Reagan was recalling their homeland and beckoning them to enlist in the fight to unite the East and West. He wasn't talking about how great America was. He wasn't selling American superiority. He wasn't teaching, cajoling, or prodding them. He wasn't talking down to them. *He was evangelizing freedom and man's spiritual heritage.* He was attempting to inspire them with soaring language and the truths that were, to him, no distant romantic dreams—but ideas related directly to them, the audience, specifically at that time in that place.

The ideas in this speech were carefully selected by Reagan to be part of a powerful message of resistance to the personal oppression of communism and the continued division of Germany. I have often wondered how many present that day might have altered their course and taken steps to help in the fight for German reunification and how many became involved in helping to bring down the Berlin Wall. Judging from the enthusiastic response from the audience to his speech, I would guess it might have changed the hearts and minds of more than a few and possibly led them toward bolder action. That was the

President's goal—to enlist more foot soldiers in his campaign to spread the message of freedom and to destroy the roots of tyranny. The results that followed just a few years afterward bear testimony to the contribution this speech might have made—along with speeches given by a small group of other leaders, few as boldly spiritual as Reagan's. That was a part of the genius of his communication—his courage, boldness, and conviction.

Another more sober and secular example of Reagan's politically evangelizing oratory was the June 1982 "Ash Heap of History," or "March of Freedom," speech delivered in Britain's imposing House of Commons. The speech came at a time of increasing tension between the United States and the Soviet Union as well as growing anxiety in Europe, and it was essential for him to lay out his rationale, his vision, and a strategy to advance democratic freedoms throughout the world. At the same time he used this historically important speech to shore up, recruit, and embolden U.S. allies to join with him in this work. To me this was one of Reagan's most complete, substantive, and intellectual addresses. As I sat in the section reserved for the White House staff directly to Reagan's left, I listened to him deliver a plan to advance freedom by masterfully according the British people the credit for being on the front lines in World War II and engaging them through his speech for a new fight against a new enemy of freedom. Here are just a few lines from a lengthy speech he delivered during an ambitious six-country, ten-day trip to Europe for the Reagans.

"What then is our course? Must civilization perish in a hail of fiery atoms? Must freedom wither in a quiet, deadening accommodation with totalitarian evil? . . . It may not be easy to see; but I believe we live now at a turning point . . . It is the Soviet Union that runs against the tide of

history . . . [It is] the march of freedom and democracy which will leave Marxism-Leninism on the ash-heap of history, as it has left other tyrannies which stifle the freedom and muzzle the self-expression of the people.

"During the dark days of the Second World War, when this island was incandescent with courage, Winston Churchill exclaimed about Britain's adversaries, 'What kind of people do they think we are?' Well, Britain's adversaries found out what extraordinary people the British are. But all the democracies paid a terrible price for allowing the dictators to underestimate us. We dare not make that mistake again. So, let us ask ourselves, 'What kind of people do we think we are?' And let us answer, 'Free people, worthy of freedom and determined not only to remain so but to help others gain their freedom as well.' "

This speech, given at the House of Commons in Westminster, was the first of a pair of two major foreign policy speeches he delivered in London. The second was the Guildhall speech, which he gave on his way back to the United States from his first visit to Moscow and his fourth meeting with Gorbachev years later. Comparing the two documents shows not only the evolution in the political environment that had occurred in the intervening six years but also a change in Reagan's tone. The first was aggressive, full of strategy, and included a call to action. The second was more a record of what was occurring as a result of this call. The *Christian Science Monitor* said of the June 1988 Guildhall presentation: "President Reagan's Guildhall speech...powerfully linked his impressions from Moscow with his convictions of a lifetime. The 'faces of hope,' the possibilities of 'lasting change' which he saw in the Soviet capital were, in his view, inseparable from the determination of Western leaders to stand by their principles." He was never at a point where he was willing to curtail his assertive oratory or, on the other hand, to even admit victory in his persistent freedom campaign for people throughout the world. Reagan's durable principles are still ready to be used for battle today with other enemies of freedom. They just need to be called upon.

Like Reagan, Churchill's speeches had included frequent use of heroic language to inspire his audiences to action. The wartime Prime Minister's stirring thirty-six-minute "Finest Hour" speech was delivered to the British House of Commons in June 1940, when Britain was in the throes of World War II, with such high drama as might have earned him an Academy Award had it been delivered on the silver screen. Churchill was conscious of the way he delivered his speeches and how they were received in war-torn Great Britain, as well as on the world stage. His work to convince the United States to join the war and help to save Western civilization was herculean, and he often called upon his vast and deep dramatic oratorical ability.

It is because of speeches like "Finest Hour" that Mr. Churchill is ranked as the most inspirational public speaker in history. He did not attain that stature easily but through a type of suffering similar to what Reagan had endured. In an *Atlantic* essay in July 1955, Isaiah Berlin wrote about Churchill in a way that gives him some resemblance to Reagan but takes a decisive turn away as well. "Churchill is acquainted with darkness as well as light. Like all inhabitants of and even transient visitors to inner worlds, he gives evidence of seasons of agonized brooding and slow recovery." While Reagan had also spent many an hour in his own neatly partitioned inner world as a young boy, he graduated from it as an optimist largely unburdened by personal chaos. Churchill had a harder climb out of darkness, while Reagan had the ladder of constant faith that helped to propel him out of it to where he eventually landed on solid ground.

During WWII, the actor Alan Hale once quipped of Reagan's loquaciousness on the back lots of film studios and at Hollywood parties, "If that [SOB] doesn't stop making speeches, he'll end up in the White House." Reagan was known in Hollywood as a big talker, but by the time he reached the White House, he had constrained his talking and subjected it to a reasonable discipline. During his presidency, he spoke millions of words, proving that big talkers can also become effective communicators through a specific set of applied skills and discipline.

Reagan, the son of a preacher, was both a born communicator and a learned one. In his very first job out of Eureka College, he won high marks in the sportscasting world. He was able to talk as fast or as slow as each play on the baseball field, and he was convincing enough to the listener to keep his audience glued to the radio. Even a skeptical Edmund Morris, the official Reagan biographer, wrote that Reagan had "the natural equipment of a sportscaster... [he had] lucidity, enthusiasm, an eye for visual detail, and a mouth that moved as fast as his mind. *Fast* is not a word most Americans today would use in remembering him, but the young Ronald Reagan could out-talk Bugs Bunny." Later Reagan won praise on the public speaking circuit by linking his political and public convictions together with his private beliefs. This potent mixture helped produce the unique Reagan brand called the Great Communicator.

According to nonagenarian A. C. Lyles, Reagan was known in Hollywood as an inveterate storyteller. He often repeated and recycled jokes and stories—to the dismay of associates— and he had the not-always-appreciated gift of gab. By the time he reached the White House, though, he had harnessed his earlier unbridled and energetic proclivity to talk too much, and he matched it with something critically important to say. Reagan knew that it is sometimes easier to talk than to be heard, and that he needed to gain the ear of his audience with a message they valued using innovative and convincing methods. As a sportscaster, Reagan had something to say that listeners wanted and were even desperate to hear, and they were thrilled by the play-by-plays he described to the rapt radio audience.

In some cases, especially when he started out reporting for radio station WHO in Des Moines, Iowa, he was not even seeing these games from the field but was reporting the play-by-play based on game developments and results that were being telegraphed or phoned to him from the playing field. He never even saw the game action with his own physical eyes. The listeners were forced to "see" the game through Reagan's imagination.

If you ever attended a Ronald Reagan speech and heard him in person, watched him on television or in a YouTube video, or even heard a recording of his voice, you may or may not have agreed with *what* he said. It would be more likely, however, that you would have agreed on how well he said it. The tone of his voice was soft and without particular stress or verbal demands. He did not yell or shout, as is the tiresome routine of some politicians and evangelists. Actually, he did not raise his voice; he modestly modulated it. He made you want to listen to him. He laid out his points confidently, supported them with facts, stories, or parables, and brought the listener into his message. Reagan adjusted his pitch and imagined, like all good communicators, that he was speaking to just one person even though his audience may have been vast. When I asked him one day about the right way to address an audience, Reagan instructed me this way:

"Find one imaginary or real person in the audience and speak directly to him while letting your eyes scan the whole audience with a broad sweep, not alighting on any one specific person, so that no one feels excluded from your verbal grasp and no one feels targeted with a fixed gaze. Don't get caught up in the feeling or fear of being overwhelmed that you are communicating with a mass of people. Imagine just speaking to one person who needs to hear what you have to say and respects it. Don't get caught up in guessing what your critics might be saying."

After Reagan taught me that, I was especially observant of his speeches to see if he followed his own advice—and of course he did.

CHAPTER SIX

Master of the Visual Image

On January 28, 1986, only seventy-three seconds after being launched from the Kennedy Space Center in Florida, the space shuttle *Challenger* exploded and fell into the Atlantic. *Challenger* carried a number of important missions, including the first teacher in space, who was to deliver lessons from her chalkboard in the sky. The nation mourned this national tragedy, especially the schoolchildren who had been prepared for Christa McAuliffe's lessons.

Reagan was also moved by this loss, and he conveyed it to the nation, delivering an inspiring televised address from the Oval Office. He shared with the mourners a vision for their loved ones that was soaring and one that called specifically for imagination and visualization. What Reagan said that day and how it moved the entire country was especially important for me, because not long after the accident, I was asked to work with those families to create a living memorial to the doomed but heroic astronauts. This program would continue the flight's mission by providing children with space science education programs on flight simulators and other inventive instructional tools. After I left the White House, I became the founding President of the Challenger Center for Space Science Education.

Here is how Reagan used his vision and imagination to console the families of the astronauts and the entire country. These remarks, masterfully written by Peggy Noonan, illustrate Reagan's special gift as a communicator, envisioning what place NASA and the *Challenger* astronauts had in history and then describing them as touching "the face of God" in his use of the magnificent poem "High Flight" by the legendary WWII aviator John Gillespie Magee.

"We'll continue our quest in space. There will be more shuttle flights and more shuttle crews and, yes, more volunteers, more civilians, more teachers in space. Nothing ends here; our hopes and our journeys continue.

"I want to add that I wish I could talk to every man and woman who works for NASA, or who worked on this mission, and tell them: 'Your dedication and professionalism have moved and impressed us for decades. And we know of your anguish. We share it.'

"There's a coincidence today. On this day 390 years ago, the great explorer Sir Francis Drake died aboard ship off the coast of Panama. In his lifetime the great frontiers were the oceans, and a historian later said, 'He lived by the sea, died on it, and was buried in it.' Well today, we can say of the Challenger *crew: Their dedication was, like Drake's, complete.*

"The crew of the shuttle Challenger *honored us by the manner in which they lived their lives. We will never forget them, nor the last time we saw them, this morning, as they prepared for their journey and waved good-bye and 'slipped the surly bonds of earth' to 'touch the face of God.' "*

Reagan frequently employed the words of the American patriot Thomas Paine, "We have it within our power to begin the world over again," as well as words from the book of Genesis, focusing specifically on the reference to man "made in the image and likeness of God." I believe that one of the most important things Reagan did was to link these two propositions for a political purpose. He felt that because man is freeborn according to Biblical authority, he is engineered for a specific purpose, and that purpose is to both enjoy his God-given freedom as well as his responsibility to make right what is wrong in society.

Reagan quoted Paine so often that many of his listeners might have actually been convinced that they *did* have the ability to begin the world over—and this was Reagan's precise purpose and hope: to empower the individual and thereby protect and strengthen American-style democracy while promoting it wherever there was the possibility of achieving it. Part of his grand strategy was to build up American-style democracy in order to bring down Soviet-style communism. To him strengthening America's confidence in its way of life was the best deterrent to the collectivist ideology that was so abhorrent to Reagan.

He knew precisely what he was doing by engaging these words and this strategy—he was uniting the American people and reinforcing the ideals and practices of democracy in the United States in order to help export it to other parts of the world. Reagan was devoted to the spirit and the letter of Paine's words, and he wanted his listeners to be as well. He saw himself as a foot soldier of the patriot, following Paine's instruction to help begin the world over again, as he felt he was doing when he committed to run for public office. Similarly, by quoting the book of Genesis, he wanted to illustrate that there was Biblical authority for the right of individual freedom. It wasn't just that he was telling people this himself; he was referencing greater authorities.

This oratorical strategy was another vehicle he used to travel over the heads of other politicians who might be in his way. If you listened to or read his speeches, this was not Reagan telling you that you were free, it was the Bible telling you that—a book he knew and respected as did a majority of American voters. Reagan drew conclusions from these truths, more than from government briefing books or government officials, and applied these to his political choices.

Reagan had the ability to envision the substance and details of what he was saying in order to help his audience see it as well—all through verbal painting, outlining, and coaching. It was said of the legendary screen actress Greta Garbo that she was so convincing in silent films because rather than simply mouthing words she found in a script, she actually thought about what they meant while she acted. She held the meaning of the script or story in her consciousness. This was proof that, as is stated by many professors of public speaking, 60 percent of all effective communication is nonverbal or unspoken.

Reagan was an actor and knew this as well. His trick was to hold the image of an event, a story, a policy, or a person in his imagination while he verbalized a description of it as vividly as possible—making the image real to the listener. He had demonstrated this skill when he called the play-by-play for baseball games he couldn't even see. This skill may well have developed for Reagan in the days when he escaped into the small attic in his parents' rented house to read, imagine, and find solitude during unpleasant episodes between his parents in the rooms below. The books he read then as a teenager— such as *Tom Sawyer*, *Huckleberry Finn*, Zane Grey's Westerns, a wide array of science fiction, and most notably the Harold Bell Wright morality tale, *That Printer of Udell's*—also helped fuel his imagination and sharpened his visualization skills, as did the plays in which he performed while in high school and college.

Reagan, in recounting his experiences at station WHO, actually called radio *"the theatre of the mind."* This ability to call a game and describe exciting or disappointing baseball plays was a special skill practiced by a few well-known men—a small troupe of colorful commentators who earned a legendary standing with radio audiences and in the sport itself. Reagan had entered a crowd that included Graham McNamee and Red Barber, who were household names at that time. Reagan was especially good at this job, and he received steady promotions as a result, until he won his first audition in Hollywood. In 1934 alone Reagan covered 140 baseball games and persuaded General Mills to sponsor him as a "telegraph commentator" for the home games of the Chicago Cubs and the White Sox. According to Myrtle Williams, the program director at Reagan's radio station, when announcers like Reagan were calling a game, "you just couldn't believe that you were not actually there. Of course he [Reagan] knew baseball and that helped."

One of the biggest selling challenges Reagan had during his presidency was to convince the public about the validity of his Strategic Defense Initiative (SDI). This approach to strategic defense, to create an impenetrable shield that would protect the United States from ballistic missile strikes launched from abroad, was a brilliant concept—although boldly futuristic at the time. For Reagan, this was an example of purposeful envisioning and imagining—envisioning the technology to make the program a reality and imagining what the outcome might be—all in order to be able to communicate its potential to the U.S. Congress and other heads of state. This initiative put Reagan squarely in the "dreamer" category—a very positive and useful character trait for the communicator and visionary leader. Through SDI he had caught the vision for making the world a safe and peaceful place by allowing not only the United States but other countries to which he offered the same technology to be immune from destruction delivered by nuclear warheads. Here is how he described his vision in 1983:

"Let me share with you a vision of the future which offers hope. It is that we embark on a program to counter the awesome Soviet missile threat with measures that are defensive. Let us turn to the very strengths in technology that spawned our great industrial base and that have given us the quality of life we enjoy today.

"What if free people could live secure in the knowledge that their security did not rest upon the threat of instant U.S. retaliation to deter a Soviet attack, that we could intercept and destroy strategic ballistic missiles before they reached our own soil or that of our allies?

"I know this is a formidable, technical task, one that may not be accomplished before the end of this century. Yet, current technology has attained a level of sophistication where it is reasonable for us to begin this effort. It will take years, probably decades, of efforts on many fronts. There will be failures and setbacks, just as there will be successes and breakthroughs. And as we proceed, we must remain constant in preserving the nuclear deterrent and maintaining a solid capability for flexible response. But isn't it worth every investment necessary to free the world from the threat of nuclear war? We know it is."

The structure of this section is especially interesting. Reagan starts by saying he wants to share something, something he has been thinking about. Next he asks the question, *"What if free people could live secure . . . ?"* Then he admits the challenges ahead and tops it off with a question that is really more a call to action. This is a perfect four-step structure for a speech based on envisioning and imagination, with the goal to bring the audience quietly to his point of view by offering to share something of value, a discovery, or a secret. He was attempting to grab the attention and stimulate the imagination in the mind of the listener. Finally, he made a call to action through a concluding question, *"But isn't it worth every investment necessary . . . ?"* He then went on to answer this question himself.

Because Reagan was a visual person, the National Security Council, and especially NSC Advisor Bud McFarlane and his staff, devised a unique and highly effective way of delivering briefings to Reagan, in advance of his meetings with foreign leaders. There were still the heavy black notebooks of preparation in advance of any meeting or trip, and Reagan conscientiously studied them; however, there was now an added tool for him to use—and it was just to Reagan's liking. This special briefing tool came in the form of videotaped reports on the people with whom he would meet. This allowed Reagan to see and learn about the personal characteristics and body language of these leaders from publicly taped speeches and talks made available by the State Department and the Pentagon.

After watching these, Reagan was able to judge the man or woman from a sense of who they were in real life, how they spoke and led—prior to when any actual meeting occurred. This preparation was the best briefing any President could ask for, and this approach uniquely suited Reagan because he could hold a visual image in his mind. It was not unlike having his own YouTube channel. He made good use of these films, watching some on Air Force One in his stateroom and office, while we in the staff would be in an adjacent lounge watching old movies or working.

Putting the Visual and Physical Image to Work

Reagan had an extraordinary White House advance team. They matched his speechwriters in their skill, and together they made a potent force. They were superior in stagecraft, the speechwriters in wordcraft. They hunted for and located innovative and dramatic venues as backdrops and speaking halls, producing exceptional lighting and sound, crowd gathering, and much more. Some of these seasoned producers had actually been trained by the Nixon advance team and had also created their own "school," which was like boot camp or basic training for new recruits to this highly skilled and creative discipline. During my years at the White House, I learned many lessons from and developed tremendous respect for members of the advance team, and I was dependent on them to make every trip and public event appear flawless. Along with the Secret Service, they made the presidency run like clockwork through their precisely timed, minute-by-minute travel and events schedules. They were like film producers on a political mission. It's no wonder that the Reagans had tremendous confidence in and appreciation for both the Secret Service and the advance teams.

Reagan also had a willingness to go into unique places to convey a message because he recognized the value of a compelling backdrop to tell a story or reinforce a visual image. I will never forget lugging piles of boxes of Federal regulations up to the Reagan ranch in Santa Barbara for him to use as an illustration when he signed the Paperwork Reduction Act next to an impressive tower of burdensome forms. I was with the Reagans when they were in Xi'an, China, being dramatically photographed with the famous Terracotta Warriors and Horses from around 200 BC during the command of the First Emperor of China. I was also with Reagan when he visited collective farms in China and engaged the farmers in small talk as they dug their furrows to plant seeds. The Reagans rarely missed communicating through photo opportunities including walking alone in Red Square then stopping their car at midnight at Arbat Street in Moscow and mingling with surprised ordinary Russians during their trip there in 1988. These were all pictures that sent a message of strong leadership and an appreciation for the richness of divergent cultures and respect for other nations. Photo ops are the stock and trade of most politicians but I thought the Reagans used them best in precisely relating the photo to a specific policy initiative or political purpose.

One of my goals in helping to plan White House foreign trips was to illustrate the Reagans' genuine interest in the history and culture of the country we were visiting. I also made a few critical mistakes in my rush to find just the right activities and venues for them to visit. For example, in thinking about our state visit to Spain, I thought—bullfighting! I knew I wanted to see it and so I thought all Americans would want to see the Reagans attending a bullfight. Wrong! There was such uproar on the part of animal rights organizations that the whole idea was quickly scrapped. On another trip, I was almost thrown out of Switzerland when I told my Swiss counterparts that we wanted to pay a visit to a drug abuse treatment center, as a part of the White House global crusade against illegal recreational drug use. The Swiss insisted that their country had no drug problem and that as a result there were no drug treatment centers in existence and thus no place for us to visit. That seemed strange to me since the main square in downtown Geneva was once known as "Needle Park." I pursued what now seems to be a slightly obnoxious tactic when I got into my own car and drove through the nearby countryside and, following leads, found a highly rated drug treatment center where we ultimately went for an official visit.

While I was on that drive, I had passed a construction site very near the headquarters of the International Red Cross, and after I had completed my mission with the drug rehab center, I drove back to see if the nearly completed building offered any opportunity. Walking around back to the construction trailer I knocked on the door and was welcomed in by an amiable and courtly gentleman, the type you would expect to be associated with an international organization of stature like the Red Cross. I plied him with questions about the new building, finding that it was to be the newly constructed Geneva headquarters of the International Red Cross Museum. It was about to be dedicated but I boldly asked them to delay their opening ceremonies by three months to coincide with the first Reagan-Gorbachev summit. Thankfully they acquiesced to my request so that those festivities were an added grace note to the 1986 Geneva Reagan-Gorbachev summit.

Another example of Reagan's use of imagery to deliver a message was the centennial celebration at the Statue of Liberty in 1986, which was rich with poignancy and again gave Reagan an opportunity to verbalize his belief once more that America is a shining city on a hill from which the rest of the world may benefit. As in any such event, the venue and the message needed to match for a message to be effectively delivered and heard. On that occasion at the feet of Lady Liberty, with the statue looming in the photo frame, Reagan said:

"We sometimes forget that even those who came here first to settle the new land were also strangers. I've spoken before of the tiny Arabella, a ship at anchor just off the Massachusetts coast. A little group of Puritans huddled on the deck. And then John Winthrop, who would later become the first Governor of Massachusetts, reminded his fellow Puritans there on that tiny deck that they must keep faith with their God, that the eyes of all the world were upon them, and that they must not forsake the mission that God had sent them on, and they must be a light unto the nations of all the world—a shining city upon a hill.

"Call it mysticism if you will, I have always believed there was some divine Providence that placed this great land here between the two great oceans, to be found by a special kind of people from every corner of the world, who had a special love for freedom and a special courage that enabled them to leave their own land, leave their friends and their countrymen and come to this new and strange land to build a New World of peace and freedom and hope."

In this speech, Reagan drew attention to and gained inspiration from the setting itself. Think of Lincoln at Gettysburg and the honor he paid that blood-soaked earth when he visited on horseback and the power he drew from that location. His oratory, enhanced by his physical travel there, has proven durable and awe-inspiring for well over a century and is considered timeless. While Reagan's settings never reached the sacred drama of Gettysburg, the intention to draw listeners to the import of the message using visual effects was a key element of every Reagan peroration.

A less elaborate but nonetheless powerful example of strategic stagecraft and image making involved a simple but intriguing switch in the side of a room in the White House where Reagan held his forty-six formal press conferences. In his eight years, Reagan gave a record number of formal press conferences, a significant accomplishment in itself, considering that today Presidents rarely hold large press conferences—where reporters are free to ask anything they like. These cumbersome historic press conferences were traditionally held in the East Room of the White House. In this iconic white-and-gold ballroom with its massive crystal chandeliers, where Presidents have hosted all kinds of events, the public also sees televised meetings and activities staged from several vantage points in the room. The way the rectangular room is physically arranged depends on the number of guests, the time of day, the particular staging required, whether or not other rooms adjacent to it would also be used, and the personal choices of the President, First Lady, and White House staff.

In many administrations, presidential press conferences were the prime opportunity for a President to answer the questions of the press corps during an hour-long session that was traditionally watched by a significant television audience. In Reagan's case, the senior staff felt that a percentage of his public approval rating and standing rested on his performance at these press conferences.

Prior to a press conference, Reagan would spend hours upon hours rehearsing in the family theatre located in the East Wing, which was usually reserved for private film screenings. In talking to reporters in the days and hours leading up to the main event, the press office would attempt to determine what questions might be asked; once they had a direction, the staff was involved in preparing fact-filled answers for the President. As for Reagan and most Presidents, they typically begin a press conference with a brief five-minute opening statement in the hope that this message will set a tone or direction for the balance of the conference. The problem was, it almost never worked. Journalists don't like to be told what they will focus on, and the press conference was mostly an opportunity for reporters and their media outlets to secure coverage for themselves on national TV. It was all highly competitive at a time when there were far fewer media outlets jockeying for their own share of the time allotted. The President would have to call on each journalist by name (a frightening challenge in itself, as the room seating and the personalities were always changing), and the show was always concluded by the "dean" of the White House press corps, who was at that time the venerable and now deceased Helen Thomas, then a UPI reporter, who had covered six presidents by the time Reagan was elected.

Reagan had one major handicap in a room like this, where these national press conferences had been held for so many years. He had a dominant strain of gentlemanliness that was hard to break. When Helen officially ended the press conference, by the iconic concluding statement "Thank You, Mr. President," it was not really over in the minds of the many journalists present. It was just a signal for revving the engines, and then the starting flag was waved for reporters to volley questions at the President, shouting over each other—even though the press conference was officially concluded and he was attempting to leave the room. In the beginning, it was easy to see that the President just could not get himself off the stage quickly enough before the journalistic stampede, and the chaotic result was a ragged ending that would immediately undo the occasional good tenor of what had gone on for an hour or more, before the official wrap-up. Reporters wanted the last word. The senior staff wanted Reagan to have the last word. There was the impasse.

Many of us encouraged the President to just walk off the stage quickly, which at that point was under a gold-draped window in the east wall of the room, and walk away—even amid the shouts of questions. Reagan, being the consummate gentleman and having been brought up to answer someone who speaks to you, could not get out of the room without fielding these verbal assaults. Something had to be done, because the contest had evolved into a competition to catch Reagan off guard and thereby create a news story for some media franchise seeking a competitive advantage.

In fairness to them, reporters complained that Reagan was far too programmed and structured, and that they never had access to him in any casual or off-the-record ways. The truth is that all journalists ask for unscripted access and few presidential staffs ever like to grant it. Yet they always ask for more access, and this is one reason they really wanted this free-for-all—to get Reagan to provide them with unpremeditated answers to their premeditated questions.

Stagecraft came to the rescue. The actual floor plan for the room was flipped. The presidential podium was moved to the opposite side of the room in front of the open doors to the main hallway—or cross hall, as it is officially referred to—from the east wall to the west, so that Reagan could enter with the grandeur of walking, on camera, the length of the red-and-gold-bordered carpet, step up to the lectern, and appear in complete control as a world leader. Then, at the end, he could elegantly and easily exit by simply turning his back and walking the same way he came in—through the grandeur and quiet of a long empty hallway—and not have to push his way through the roaring, questioning, soliciting crowd. This was a genius idea and was typical of the way the Reagan White House made attempts to control the message and the staging—and succeeded in a majority of cases.

Today there are more diverse ways for a President to communicate a message. In our Administration, we also sought ways to lessen the dependence on what now seem to be antiquated vehicles for communication—like the major press conference. That is one reason the President's weekly Saturday morning radio address was inaugurated—and is a tradition that continues today. This gave Reagan and subsequent presidents a small window of time to talk directly to the American people without being interrupted at all.

Remaining in Control When Challenged

When we traveled to Portugal for a 1985 state visit as a part of a five-country European tour, Reagan was invited to deliver an address at the Portuguese National Congress in Lisbon. The focus of the speech was Portugal's burgeoning democracy and his praise for its then eleven-year record. The presentation, which I could observe from my seat in the massive domed chamber, was progressing very well until protestors, leftists, and communists entered the ornate and historic room and released white doves to fly around the space as a distraction to Reagan's speech. Reagan's instinctive response was to take control of the event, while attempting to win the audience back by showing that he was not unnerved by this surprise and making them feel at ease.

As a result, he was able to turn the protest to his advantage

and refocus the audience on his message. He noted that protests like these were a *"part of the democratic process,"* but added
with a note of sarcastic humor, *"I'm sorry that the seats on the left
seem to be uncomfortable."* Then he turned back to his text with
a compelling story about meeting with the Pope and talking
with him about the Portuguese shrine of Fatima. He continued, *"I dared to suggest that in the example of men like himself [the
Pope], and in the prayers of simple people everywhere—simple people
like the children of Fatima—there resides more power than in all the
great armies and statesmen of the world."*

Reagan always attempted to conquer the unanticipated
and untoward question without reacting in fear. Watching
him take control of an unexpected and unfriendly question
was one of the most important lessons I learned about communication. Reagan thought that tough questions should be
welcomed—and actually encouraged—because they helped
clarify the ideas being communicated. Reagan was not always
fast on his feet in a rugged questioning session, but he knew
enough not to surrender the podium in weakness.

I remember asking Margaret Thatcher, another master of
stagecraft, why she was such an effective public speaker. She
told me: "You never completely lose the fear, no, never. Sometimes when I reach the podium I have to say to myself, 'Come
on, old gal, you can do it.' But that little bit of fear always
sticks with you, and the energy you derive from it gives you
more courage to press onward with what you have to say."

Reagan didn't always have the perfect rejoinder at the ready
when challenged, but he did not appear to be fearful of his
audiences, however threatening and ready to parry they might
have been. I also learned from him that a direct question does
not necessarily have to be directly answered. When faced with

an untoward question, Reagan might use the questioner's frame of reference but respond with something he wanted the audience to hear—not necessarily what the questioner was seeking. Never lose control and never repeat the negative question to buy time. These are among the many critical laws of effective communication that I learned from the Reagans.

On a couple of memorable occasions, Reagan demonstrated his ability to turn the challenge away by not actually answering the question but by cleverly deflecting it when, for example, President Carter charged that candidate Reagan "began his political career campaigning against Medicare," in an attempt to indict him for a position that would cause him to lose his standing with senior citizens. Reagan's quip back had nothing to do with the charge. Instead he deflected it with his now iconic response, *"Now there you go again!"*—meaning by that, "Mr. Carter, you have been speaking untruths all evening and here is another one!"

This happened at the 1980 Cleveland presidential debate. My wife and I were sitting in the tenth row of the audience, and you could see that even Carter was smiling at Reagan's besting him. Seasoned journalist and Reagan biographer Lou Cannon wrote of this incident that Reagan's "response was funny, irreverent, and thoroughly authentic. It did not answer Carter's point, but it revealed a functioning intellect."

Reagan did something similar when asked, in a 1984 debate, whether he was too old to be president. Rather than answering that question directly, Reagan delivered one of his best one-liners—and put to rest not only the issues about his age, but diminished somewhat the candidacy of Walter Mondale. *"I have decided I will not make age an issue in this campaign,"* he replied. *"Therefore I am not going to exploit, for political purposes, my opponent's youth and inexperience."* The audience howled as he hit that one out of the ballpark. Even Mondale was grinning.

Reagan had an ideal disposition for handling hostile and challenging questions. He did not have a temper and he genuinely liked people, despite the fact that they might not have liked him or wanted to use him for political target practice. He did not react—that is, he had a long fuse and did not lose control. Few people in leadership positions have such a thick skin, but he taught me not to react to, compete with, or disparage competitors, especially those in the media. Doing that would allow them to take control of the message. In addition, fighting back could turn your opponents against you more fiercely, and your allies may begin to question your veracity as well.

Reagan often advised me to "Be a well and not a fount" when referring to the assertively inquiring media. What he meant by that was that I should be a well, or source of information, but that I shouldn't spout unnecessary details in an undisciplined way unless asked specifically for them—and perhaps not even then. He knew that being placed in a stressful interview with a journalist often causes you to start offering up more information than is necessary; furthermore, it is a journalist's job to make you so comfortable that you will do precisely that. If you can picture Reagan in an interview, you would have observed that Reagan followed this advice himself. He was a master at being a well.

Another Reagan tactic was to recall, when challenged, the main message he was conveying and to not deviate from it, making every attempt to weave or reweave the original points into his reply. Reagan always attempted to remain in control of the presentation and message, even though this frustrated the media. He provided useful information, recognizing that a journalist has a job to do. This is what Reagan always attempted to do. It was his operating principle. He did not react to taunts. He did not surrender the podium. This added strength to the presidency.

Using Emotion Economically

There were times Reagan was moved to tears, although he typically held those in check. This conveyed that he was emotional or moved about what he was saying or about the details surrounding an event, but that he had the strength to control the emotion. He knew that expressing emotion reveals the speaker's vulnerability in a positive way and helps unite the audience with him. Yet he also knew that tears can evoke weakness, too, as some unfortunate politicians have learned the hard way.

When in doubt, Reagan exercised restraint. He knew that there is a distinction between the audience being moved by the words spoken, and an undisciplined focus on the individual speaker and his own problems, memories, or connections to an event, or situation. Tears, as sincere as they might be, could also be considered a sign of instability.

There was a great deal of emotion in evidence when Reagan attended the June 1984 fortieth anniversary of D-day at Pointe du Hoc in Normandy, France. Reagan was of the age when he himself might have actually landed on French soil that horrific day—and he could have, if he had not been kept from action due to very poor eyesight. His love of country and respect for his countrymen who fought there all came together at that celebration. I had the privilege of advancing this trip and also accompanying Nancy Reagan when she was invited to be the honored guest at the thirty-eighth anniversary of D-day, two years before the President would attend. There is no more haunting site than the Allied cemeteries in Normandy, indelibly marking the human costs of WWII and the fight against tyranny by what the television journalist and author Tom Brokaw called the Greatest Generation.

The location, the presence of the other heads of state, and the festivities themselves produced an ample amount of emotion and Reagan's remarks solemnly reflected that. His speech has been titled, "The Boys of Pointe du Hoc," and it was especially but not exclusively dedicated to a few of the veterans who traveled to be present at the anniversary ceremony. These were the men who fought at Omaha Beach in a group called the Rangers, 225 strong at the launch of the invasion, with ninety survivors at the end of the first day of fighting. Reagan spoke directly to them as well as to a broader audience when he said, in part:

"Forty summers have passed since the battle that you fought here. You were young the day you took these cliffs; some of you were hardly more than boys with the deepest joys of life before you. Yet you risked everything here. Why? Why did you do it? What impelled you to put aside the instinct for self-preservation and risk your lives to take these cliffs? . . . We look at you and somehow we know the answer. It was faith and belief; it was loyalty and love.

"The men of Normandy had faith that what they were doing was right, faith that they fought for all humanity, faith that a just God would grant them mercy on this beachhead or on the next. It was the deep knowledge—and pray God we have not lost it—that there is a profound, moral difference between the use of force for liberation and the use of force for conquest. You were here to liberate, not to conquer, and

so you and those others did not doubt your cause. And you were right not to doubt.

"You all knew that some things are worth dying for. One's country is worth dying for, and democracy is worth dying for, because it's the most deeply honorable form of government ever devised by man. All of you loved liberty. All of you were willing to fight tyranny, and you knew the people of your countries were behind you.

"The Americans who fought here that morning knew word of the invasion was spreading through the darkness back home. They fought— or felt in their hearts, though they couldn't know in fact, that in Georgia they were filling the churches at 4 a.m., in Kansas they were kneeling on their porches and praying, and in Philadelphia they were ringing the Liberty Bell.

"Something else helped the men of D-day: their rock-hard belief that Providence would have a great hand in the events that would unfold here; that God was an ally in this great cause. And so, the night before the invasion, when Colonel Wolverton asked his parachute troops to kneel with him in prayer he told them: 'Do not bow your heads, but look up so you can see God and ask His blessing in what we're about to do.' Also that night, General Matthew Ridgway on his cot, listening in the darkness for the promise God made to Joshua: 'I will not fail thee nor forsake thee.'

"These are the things that impelled them; these are the things that shaped the unity of the Allies."

These remarks, and the whole body of Reagan's text, drew upon the remarkable details of what happened on the stark cliffs June 6, 1944, and were delivered with Reagan's own interpretation of what also went on in the hearts and minds of these veterans. In this speech he effectively used emotion to teach and to say, in effect, "I know why these veterans fought, and it was because of the beliefs and values the world needs more of now." He used the feeling of the occasion to convey with words what he felt the world needed to pay attention to in our time—not just for history. Reagan used emotion intentionally. He did not let emotion use him.

There was also emotion and pride in Reagan's remarks to the U.S. medal winners at the 1984 Los Angeles Olympic Games. When talking about heroism, he said:

"The specialness of this Olympics was apparent from the beginning. You walked into the opening ceremonies with a special kind of pride, a vibrant and a very human delight that was transmitted to the crowds and that was picked up by the people who were watching on TV. Throughout the games, I couldn't help but think that if the people of the world judged Americans by what they saw of you, then they might think, 'Americans? Well, they're generous and full of serious effort; they're full of high spirits; they're motivated by all the best things. They're truly a nation of champions.'"

Here was Reagan again telling people how good they are, giving people a sense of fulfillment and of feeling good about themselves as capable of achieving something.

Reagan could also be playful, and, of course, he loved hearing and telling jokes. He was well known for using humor in his speeches alongside other, more serious, elements. Most of Reagan's public humor was deployed in a self-deprecating way and rarely at another's expense. His humor was also purposeful in that it was typically used to support or illustrate a specific point of policy or to reinforce his beliefs. An example of this could be found in Reagan's repeated use of age in a playful way. This was masterful because Reagan was, in reality, the oldest person to be elected president, and his critics thought to use this to their own advantage. Reagan, however, used it to his advantage in a way that the audience could say, "Oh, of course age is not an issue for him." He referred many times to having had conversations with the Founding Fathers or leaders from an earlier time, implying impossibly great age. He said,

"Thomas Jefferson once said . . . 'We should never judge a president by his age, only by his works.' And ever since he told me that, I stopped worrying."

Reagan was cautious and careful about using humor in public, but privately he was eclectic in his taste in humor. P. J. O'Rourke, the prolific writer and humorist, wrote of Reagan's joking this way: "Ronald Reagan has a sense of proportion, a sense of how life is and always will be . . . President Reagan understands the 'humors,' the ruling passions, that beset men and institutions . . . And, as with all great humorists, Ronald Reagan can go to the heart of a matter with precision and brevity that shame drab think-tankers . . . Ready wit makes Ronald Reagan a tough opponent. And wit that tells the truth is hard to parry."

Reagan used targeted humor to not so subtly malign the Soviet Union, government bureaucracy in the United States, and a few other pointed favorites. These stories sounded harmless, but they were designed to make a point and stick with you, the way humor usually does. Some were used to warm up the audience and relieve any tension in the room before starting in on a serious speech. In every case, Reagan used stories as a device to make a connection with the audience that was nonthreatening and to create a bond with his listeners. Here is an example of how he used humor to further a political goal:

"And there's a story about a Russian and an American who were talking about the freedoms in their countries; and the American said, 'Listen, in America,' he said, 'I can stand on any street corner or out in the park or anyplace I want and openly criticize the President of the

United States.' And the Russian said, 'We have the same privilege in the Soviet Union.' And the American was pretty surprised. [The Russian said,] 'I can stand on any street corner in any park in Russia, and I can openly criticize the President of the United States.' "

This type of targeted, purposeful humor was another way for Reagan to make a point. James Denton, editor of *Grinning with the Gipper*, a useful collection of Reagan's jokes, tells of going to the White House for a briefing one day and realizing that there was purpose in Reagan's humor and stories. He writes, "I was first struck by Ronald Reagan's masterful use of humor while [I was] attending a briefing on tax reform at the White House at which the President spoke—several months into his second term. He was on a roll: *'There are some in government who have a very simple tax proposal in mind. There will be only two lines on the tax form: How much did you make last year? Send it.'* Then a couple of months later, at a similar occasion there he was again, warming up his audience with a fresh comedy routine which made him impossible not to like. But what is more, somehow this President of the United States was making each person out there feel that he liked them personally. That was Ronald Reagan. He had mastered the standup comedy routine in Las Vegas, earlier in his career. But now on a larger stage he added meaning to it and delivered it purposely to the hearts and minds of Americans."

Reagan's personality was a key to his delivery of both humor and emotion. He let the words—the story, the parable, the quotation, and the joke—do the work.

CHAPTER SEVEN

Man of Faith in a Secular Pulpit

Every day the correspondence unit at the White House, located in the adjacent massive gray wedding-cake-style Victorian structure known now as the Eisenhower Executive Office Building, receives thousands of letters, e-mails, texts, tweets, and other forms of communication from constituents. The staff, many of whom are volunteers, have various ways of handling their responses. During our time there, they would randomly select letters for the President to review personally. These were a sampling of letters from Americans they thought would be meaningful for him to see. Some of these writers received handwritten responses directly from the President. The same was true for the First Lady. The correspondence office staff also sought specific detailed information from all of us on the senior staff in order to be able to answer these letters correctly.

One day a member of the correspondence office asked me if I knew the President's favorite hymns or if he even had any. Apparently someone had written to the White House to find out. I think I was asked this question because they assumed I would ask the First Lady and she would know the answer. I

144

decided, however, to ask the President directly. I was pleas-antly surprised to hear him tell me that two of his favorites were also favorites of my dad, who also very much enjoyed hymn singing.

The first was "In the Garden" and the second was "Sweet Hour of Prayer." When he told me his choices, I was impressed. Then, to my surprise and enjoyment, he quietly sang them to me. He had all the words committed to memory, and I thought he prob-ably referred to them and actually depended on them regularly, albeit privately. He didn't refer to a hymnal when answering my question; he referred to his memory and his heart. He knew right away how he would answer my question, did not hesitate, and quietly responded—lyrically. I did not think of Reagan as musi-cal or as having a particularly good singing voice, and he did not prove me wrong when he sang me these hymns. He added that there were many other hymns he liked as well. Of course I wanted to continue our conversation about hymns much lon-ger; however, our vocal experience was sandwiched in between meetings and was cut short. Hymn singing was a part of the wor-ship service in his boyhood church and on the campus of Eureka College—which was church affiliated, so Reagan would have heard these hymns and sung them regularly for many years. The fact that he sung the hymns to me was not only delightful and moving—imagine being sung to by the President of the United States!—but was proof that his answer was not superficial. He knew and loved these hymns and put them to use.

After this brief, impromptu concert up in the family quar-ters, I went back to my office and researched the words of both hymns, and I thought about what they might have meant to Reagan and why he selected those to share with me. The first hymn, "In the Garden," seemed especially to fit with my view of Reagan and his relationship with God—especially because the chorus contains these words: "And He walks with me, and He talks with me / And He tells me I am His own; / And the joy we share as we tarry there, / None other has ever known." Here, I thought, was the center of Reagan's belief system; a walk with God, a talk with God. Personal. Private. Learned from his mother. Depended upon in boyhood. Tested in adversity. Reagan had a walk with God to the degree I had never seen in anyone else—and I have met and known many God-fearing and prayerful people in my life. It was quiet and confident. That was what he kept inside. That was what he kept as unknowable and unshared with the outside world. This was the essence of the man—not his intellect, although surely he had a fine one, but his spiritual perspective, his walk with his God. This was the inner force that animated him, directed him, spoke to him, comforted him, and allowed him to be that contained and complete individual who in some ways did not need anyone else—despite his closeness to and dependence on his wife.

Perhaps, considering Reagan's hymnbook favorites, he used these as prayers in a way that my daughter Lauren once referred to in reply to a friend who had asked her what it meant to pray: "Prayer is easy," she told her friend. "It's just like singing."

There were a couple of occasions where Reagan did reveal publicly what he prayed for. We do know that while he was recovering from his bullet wound at the George Washington University Hospital, he was praying for his would-be assassin—probably among many other things that he did not specifically mention or record. In his youth he had seen his mother heal people through prayer, so this might have been a time he used her example in his own life. Reagan's diaries and his autobiography are filled with numerous references to praying, and some even mention the names of people he prayed for including, interestingly, his own father-in-law, the noted and formidable Chicago neurosurgeon, Dr. Loyal Davis—whose Phoenix funeral I managed for the Reagans in 1982.

People across a broad spectrum of the public say they pray—most notably in crisis—but many also talk about regular daily prayer. In fact, according to Barna Research, 84 percent of Americans pray at least once per week, and 64 percent say they pray more than once a day. If these statistics are a correct reflection of the general voting population, I would imagine that those who pray would expect their leaders to pray as well. As Reagan noted in 1984 at the Dallas Prayer Breakfast:

"The Mayflower Compact began with the words: 'In the name of God, amen.' The Declaration of Independence appeals to 'Nature's God' and 'the Creator' and 'the Supreme Judge of the world.' Congress was given a chaplain, and the oaths of office are oaths before God."

Faith was a strong strain in Reagan's character, and it was interwoven with every other element in it. Faith for Reagan was no Sunday occurrence. His elements of faith were fundamental to who he was as a human being, leader, and communicator. They were the simple reality of the man and the largest aspect of his individuality. His leadership and communication abilities were the direct result of this integrated and integral core.

Reagan was not the only American leader for whom faith has been a dominant element of character, as he himself pointed out again at the same Dallas Prayer Breakfast when he referred to the religious ideals of the Founding Fathers:

"James Madison in the Federalist Papers *admitted that in the creation of our Republic he 'perceived the hand of the Almighty.' John Jay, the first Chief Justice of the Supreme Court, warned we must never forget the 'God from whom our blessing flowed.' George Washington*

referred to religion's 'profound and unsurpassed place in the heart of our nation.' And Washington voiced reservations about the idea that there could be a wise policy without a firm and moral and religious foundation. He said, 'Of all the dispositions and habits which lead to political prosperity, religion and morality are indispensable supports.' "

In a study of the Founding Fathers and their faith published by the Lehrman Institute, political scientist John G. West Jr. is quoted as saying that George Washington's "political theology was far from ambiguous. It incorporated three great propositions ... First, Washington believed that religion served as the necessary defender of morality in civic life. Second, he maintained that the moral law defended by religion was the same moral law that can be known by reason. Third, he saw religious liberty as a natural right of all human beings."

Historian Samuel Eliot Morison also wrote of the first American President, "He believed in God ... He was certain of a Providence in the affairs of men. By the same token, he was completely tolerant of other people's beliefs, more so than the American democracy of today; for in a letter to the Swedenborgian church of Baltimore he wrote: 'In this enlightened age and in the land of equal liberty it is our belief that a man's religious tenets will not forfeit the protection of the law, nor deprive him of the right of attaining and holding the highest offices that are known in the United States.' But Washington never became an active member of any church."

Similarly, John Adams was a believer. Historian Edwin S. Gaustad wrote: "From early entries in his diary to letters written late in life, Adams composed variations on a single theme: God is so great, I am so small. Adams never doubted who was in charge of the universe, never believed himself as master of his, or anyone's destiny."

In 1846 <u>Abraham Lincoln wrote,</u> "That I am not a member of any Christian Church, is true; but I have never denied the truth of the Scriptures; and I have never spoken with intentional disrespect of religion in general, or any denomination of Christians in particular... <u>I do not think I could myself, be</u> <u>brought to support a man for office, whom I knew</u> to be an <u>open enemy of, and scoffer at, religion.</u>"

Jimmy Carter was a Baptist who taught Sunday School in his hometown of Plains, Georgia, and in Washington after he was elected President. Carter called himself a born-again Christian. Carter said that as President he prayed every day. After his time in office he published a study Bible as well as Sunday School lessons, and he said that he read a passage of Scripture every night aloud, taking turns with his wife, Rosalynn.

George W. Bush, also a professed born-again Christian and Methodist, was also very public and forthcoming with his profession of faith. When Bush was running for president, he was asked his favorite political philosopher. He famously answered, "Jesus Christ—because he changed my heart."

In March 1981, Reagan wrote in his Proclamation for a National Day of Prayer,

"Prayer is today as powerful a force in our nation as it has ever been. We as a nation should never forget this source of strength. And while recognizing that the freedom to choose a godly path is the essence of liberty, as a Nation we cannot but hope that more of our citizens would, through prayer, come into a closer relationship with their Maker."

What is unusual here is not that there was such a proclamation, because speechwriters have been crafting these messages for decades. It was what this proclamation stood for: <u>recognizing</u> the power of prayer and the need of more Americans to have a relationship with God through prayer. I can only conjecture, but having known him I can imagine that Ronald Reagan prayed for this eventuality.

Reagan said publicly that he believed in intercessory prayer. He said that at times he also had the actual sensation of being prayed for by others. He talked of how grateful he was that people were praying for him, and it helped him do his job better. In October 1983 he said,

"Hardly a day goes by that I'm not told—sometimes in letters and sometimes by people that I meet and perfect strangers—and they tell me that they're praying for me. Well, thanks to [my mother] Nelle Reagan, I believe in intercessory prayer, I know that those prayers are giving me strength that I would not otherwise possess."

He told the story that while Governor of California, he was visited one afternoon by two different groups of people lobbying him for something on behalf of their constituents. Before each one left the state capitol building they suddenly ran back into his office and told Reagan they were praying for him. He was deeply affected by that. Shortly after this he found, while visiting his doctor, that a diagnosed stomach ailment from which he had been suffering, and receiving regular medical treatment for, had completely disappeared. This was confirmed by his physician. Reagan attributed this healing to the power of prayer and of those seeking it for him while he was in public office.

To talk openly about prayer should not be difficult in a free and open society; however, in relationship to politics, it is a tricky thing to do. Prayer is subjective, taught in various ways, and practiced in even more. It can be used to justify going to war and inflicting harm as well as being used to heal, find solace, seek guidance, and save lives. When it comes to leaders, most of them will profess a proclivity to pray, and they will admit to doing so but will wisely leave the particulars out of most discussions. Private prayer is what we are talking about here. Public prayer practiced in churches, in synagogues, or in mosques, or on hillsides or street corners is something else. Most American Presidents have admitted the need for prayer and have written and talked publicly about it, some more openly than others. Reagan said that he had learned from his mother *"the value of prayer, how to have dreams and believe I could make them come true."*

Presidents since Eisenhower have always attended the traditional National Prayer Breakfast usually held in February in Washington each year—an event held in the largest ballroom in the nation's capital. This event has grown significantly since its establishment in 1953 as the Presidential Prayer Breakfast to become an international event with a long waiting list of those who seek to be admitted as guests. I have heard some surprising confessionals and genuinely humble and personal introspections voiced at these breakfasts by celebrities and national officeholders—which makes the interlude at that breakfast seem so refreshing.

At Reagan's first Prayer Breakfast appearance, he told the now-popularized parable that he liked so much that I heard him repeat it several times. The story goes that as a man was walking on the beach, he turned to look back and saw two sets of footprints in the sand where he had been walking—except that in intervals, there was only one set of footprints. Seeing these intervals as times of trouble in his life, he asked God to explain why He was not walking alongside of him—as God had promised always to do. It was then that God explained, "During those times of trouble, my son, there was only one set of footprints in the sand because I was carrying you."

I think Reagan actually saw himself as the man on the

beach. It was a metaphor for his life and how he had always lived it. He needed God at his side and felt Him there. He could describe this walk in parables like this one but rarely talked about it to others in personal terms.

At another Prayer Breakfast he said:

"I'm so thankful that there will always be one day in the year when people all over our land can sit down as neighbors and friends and remind ourselves of what our real task is. This task was spelled out in the Old and the New Testament. Jesus was asked, 'Master, which is the great commandment in the law?' And He replied, 'Thou shalt love the Lord thy God with all thy heart, and with all thy soul, and with all thy mind. This is the first and great commandment. The second is like unto it, thou shalt love thy neighbor as thyself. On these two commandments hang all the law and the prophets.'"

And he himself confessed at another one of these annual events,

"I've always believed that we were, each of us, put here for a reason, that there is a plan, somehow a divine plan for all of us. I know that whatever days are left to me belong to Him."

Lincoln was also especially candid in his writing and talking about his need for prayer and how often he resorted to it. Washington is said to have prayed before every battle. Eisenhower talked about praying all through World War II and his presidency. Because praying most always refers to silent communion or meditation, it is a right of the individual that can never be taken away—and Reagan referred to it in this way. Reagan also liked to refer to Lincoln and recount that during his struggles to end slavery and reunite the country he would often drop to his knees in prayer because he had "nowhere else to go." Reagan also said on the National Day of Prayer in 1982,

"The most sublime picture in American history is of George Wash-

ington on his knees in the snow at Valley Forge. That image personifies a people who know that it's not enough to depend on our own courage and goodness; we must also seek help from God, our Father and Preserver."

It says a lot about Reagan that he called this painting the *"most sublime"* picture—a picture painted in 1975 by artist Arnold Friberg, who also painted the illustrations used in the epic motion picture film *The Ten Commandments*. Others may disagree on its relative importance as a painting, but they cannot disagree that this is how Reagan saw the imagery.

Reagan told of praying before beginning most meetings and before every airplane flight—which was not unlike how he prayed before every football game he played in college. Prior to one Cabinet meeting, an official suggested to the President that the group institute a new practice of beginning each meeting with everyone praying. Turning to Reagan for approval, he was surprised to hear the President respond sparsely and poignantly, "Oh, I already have," and then he continued on with the business at hand.

I feel this story is significant in illustrating Reagan's religious practice and inner spirit. To him prayer was quiet and personal, not something for public display. While there were times in his life that he did pray in a group, he did not typically call on others to join him. He must have known intuitively that praying in public, especially when you are an elected politician, can lead to stereotypes not always helpful to the political process. During my time in the White House a group of senior staff members organized a weekly prayer breakfast in the staff dining room, called the Mess, which I occasionally attended and enjoyed, and from which I benefited. I do not ever recall seeing the President there, although he was invited and may have attended once or twice. This was just not his route to praying as President.

There was one time, however, where a special type of prayer got noisy. The Reagans hosted a regular Public Broadcasting System arts and entertainment show known as *In Performance at the White House*. It featured leading artists from all genres and had a different theme each year. I served as the internal producer and primary contact for the team of outside producers for the show. One year the focus was on American music, and we decided to take the telecast outside the White House for the segment on American gospel music. I scoured Washington for the best gospel choir and music director and found them at a very special inner-city church. After the official taping was concluded, the music continued to roll and the Reagans got up on the stage and danced and sang spontaneously. They enjoyed the freedom of the moment and the great sound of the gospel music, which went on for some time before we realized we had better let the church shut down and let the congregants go home—which we finally did, as well.

The most moving story to me about Reagan and prayer was told by Judge William Clark, who some considered to be Reagan's best friend and was someone I deeply respected. Bill Clark was Reagan's first National Security Advisor and later Secretary of the Interior and had been with him during his years as Governor of California. It is retold in this way in Paul Kengor's enlightening book *God and Ronald Reagan*. In 1968 Clark and Reagan were traveling across the country on a TWA flight. A shaken "Clark informed the governor that Martin Luther King, Jr., had been shot. He expected some comment from Reagan in return, but heard nothing. Clark stepped away; when he turned back around he found Reagan in prayer, looking down at his knees, lips moving in silence."

Also reported in Kengor's book is Clark's recounting of how

he often stood by Reagan in the Oval Office when he called the families of servicemen and servicewomen who had been killed in active duty, adding that it was Reagan's practice to always say, "Shall we say a little prayer together?" They would always say yes. And then Reagan would lead an audible prayer with them and for them. Kengor also shared with me how these two men, Clark and Reagan, carried on a quiet secret code they used when troubling news of some kind reached the White House. Both men knew when prayer was needed and they would instinctively remind each other by saying quietly, "DP"—meaning "Divine Providence"—to acknowledge the need to reach out to this Power for help. At the 1980 Republican Convention in Detroit, Reagan dramatically revealed how he felt about prayer. In accepting the nomination of his party, he concluded his remarks this way:

"I'll confess that I've been a little afraid to suggest what I'm going to suggest—I'm more afraid not to—that we begin our crusade joined together in a moment of silent prayer."

His request was met with a stark quiet throughout the cavernous hall and Reagan ended it all a few minutes later with the way he always liked to sign off—*"God bless America"*—and then he was off on his campaign, which ultimately took him to the White House.

A Man of Faith

Barbara Walters, the iconic television journalist, was once invited to the Reagan ranch, Rancho del Cielo, or Heaven's Ranch, in the Santa Ynez Mountains high above Santa Barbara for one of her televised interviews with Reagan. They sat outside, because the modest adobe ranch house was too small for the film crew to fit inside. Reagan had built the house himself with the help of a few ranch hands. Walters, with the cameras rolling, asked the President what he liked most about life on the ranch. First he talked about going there in the thick of worrisome world problems and finding solace. Then he pointed to the sweeping, majestic view of the Pacific and, with a broad gesture of his hand panning over the magnificent 360-degree view, said that this vista always gave him solace and reminded him of the Bible phrase from Psalm 121, *"I will lift up mine eyes unto the hills, from whence cometh my help. My help cometh from the Lord."*

Reagan did not make this reference on national television casually or to win votes. It was not written for him by speechwriters or supplied on a teleprompter. It came naturally to him, and he had obviously thought about it many times when moving around the ranch, clearing brush and chopping wood as he liked to do.

Reagan, who loved to ride at the ranch, often said, *"There is nothing so good for the mind of a man than the back of a horse."* The agents on his security detail, like John Barletta and earlier Dennis LeBlanc, a former California State Trooper, who had guarded Reagan as Governor, became riding friends, and they could attest to how much Reagan appreciated his rides especially while he was President, and how he used this time in his own meditative way to think about and plan his next moves politically.

Reagan knew his Bible. It sat on the night table next to his bed right alongside the secure phone, which frequently awakened him in the night with news of a crisis somewhere in the world. His Bible was big and old and worn out. Apparently he wanted it that way, because he was certainly sent many new ones by well-meaning people who thought he should read it more. I was frequently asked if I could pass along to the President some religious tract or a Bible—thinking that Reagan might not be acquainted with it!

What most of these people and the general public did not know then was that he had been a Sunday School teacher who never missed a 9:30 a.m. class on Sunday, followed by a youth service. In fact when he attended Eureka College he drove the one hundred miles north to his hometown of Dixon to teach every single Sunday. One of his closest friends in Dixon went off to divinity school, and Reagan thought for a while about going with him. His girlfriend from high school through college was the preacher's daughter, Margaret Cleaver, whom he expected to marry and whose father served as surrogate father for Reagan, taught him to drive a car, and recommended him for enrollment at Eureka College.

Having been in and out of the Reagans' bedroom many times, where the First Lady worked daily at an old mahogany kneehole desk, I had often noticed the Bible next to his bed. I decided I would ask him about it and if he actually read it. *"Oh, yes,"* he said, *"and sometimes in the middle of the night."* Then he took me over to the large, worn, leather book and pointed out specific references handwritten in the front of the book and some of the passages in Psalms and elsewhere that had been underlined for quick reference. Examining that book, I saw that it had been put to good use. It was not a fancy, beautifully bound, hand-tooled volume sitting high up on a bookshelf. It was right where he could reach for it. Then while we were talking about it, he stopped and read me two or three passages that were favorites of his—mostly ones of comfort and guidance from the Psalms and Isaiah—again proof that he knew the text and could easily turn to the passages that had helped him. It was an extraordinary privilege for me to be read the Bible by the President of the United States.

Reagan thoroughly identified with the practical Christianity, good works, and relaxed liturgy of the Disciples of Christ Church where he was baptized on June 21, 1922. He was active in this church through his college years, joining in youth activities and in his Sunday School teaching. Reagan later joined the Hollywood Presbyterian Church, and years after that, the Bel Air Presbyterian Church when it was organized and where he remained a member for more than thirty years. He did not officially join the large and modern National Presbyterian Church when he came to Washington, DC. However, he did worship there several times, took communion from its pastor, and was engaged with the pastoral staff.

Worshipping in a church on Sunday was always problematic for the Reagans. When they lived in California, they would often spend weekends at their ranch or might be traveling out of the area. During the eight years of his governorship the Reagans frequently commuted on weekends between Sacramento and Los Angeles. Then during their White House years and especially following the assassination attempt, security was significantly increased. If the President were to attend a church service, everyone in the congregation would be required to pass through magnetometers or metal detectors like at an airport. This precluded his church attendance without disrupting the service and moving the focus from the pulpit to the President. Reagan said he was uncomfortable with that, and so he forfeited attendance. Some critics had a problem with the Reagans' lack of church attendance—if for no other reason than a President should set an example for the country. Had I not known of Reagan's deep and personal spiritual convictions, as so many did not, I would have shared this concern—even though church attendance would not necessarily be an accurate way to judge a person's genuine spiritual commitment.

Like so many of his predecessors, Reagan hosted the world-renowned evangelist and preacher Billy Graham at the White House. Reverend Donn Moomaw, from his home church in Bel Air, also visited the White House on several occasions and officiated at both inaugurations. Reagan also called on John Boyles, an associate pastor at the National Presbyterian Church in Washington, for counsel.

After he left office, Reagan and Boyles were in communication about Boyles' submission to the *Washington Post* of the President's first Christmas address to the nation, which featured in the opening section the story of the birth of Jesus. Boyles had been pleased that the paper published the address but disappointed that they edited out the first part, which was the most religious. Years after leaving office, Reagan read this story in the National Presbyterian Church bulletin and wrote Boyles a handwritten note of appreciation from his Los Angeles office. He thanked him for having even submitted his message to the *Post* in the first place. As Boyles related to me personally, he was taken aback with the fact that Reagan was reading the church bulletin, much less responding to him in such a personal and focused way.

For Reagan the main idea in his practice of Christianity was his subordination to Divine Providence. This gave him not only a sense of security and direction but a desire for service, and a way to keep his personal ambitions in check with what God wanted him to do and to be. It also immunized him, in a way, from the egotism that can swell and swallow, almost unknowingly, any leader. This is the way a *Washington Times* editorial characterized Reagan's faith and its impact in his job:

"The faith was a part of all his words. In his 'Time for Choosing' speech, Mr. Reagan declared, *'We'll preserve for our children this, the last best hope of man on Earth, or we will sentence them to take the last step into a thousand years of darkness.'* In his first inaugural address, he said, *'I'm told that tens of thousands of prayer meetings are being held on this day, and I'm deeply grateful. We are a nation under God, and I believe God intended us to be free.'*

"His works reflected his faith as well. He spoke against abortion and for prayer in schools. He transformed cultural conservatism's frown at vice into a smile at virtue. Mr. Reagan returned unapologetic patriotism to the national discourse; he restored personal freedom and responsibility as the touchstones of the national philosophy. While he saw moral courage as an essential weapon of free men, he made sure that the Cold Warriors were well-armed and well-equipped."

Most leaders, including U.S. Presidents, are defined and measured by their achievements under pressure or as the result of some sort of national or personal adversity. After Reagan was shot and while he was recuperating, he wrote in his diary:

"Whatever else happens now, I owe my life to God and will try to serve Him in every way I can."

He also said, speaking of his would-be assassin:

"I realized I couldn't ask for God's help while at the same time I felt hatred for the mixed-up angry young man who had shot me. Isn't that the meaning of the lost sheep? We are all God's children and therefore equally loved by Him. I began to pray for his soul and that he would find his way back into the fold."

At Reagan's burial site, in Simi Valley, California, there is an engraved epitaph containing words Reagan wrote that reveals a great deal about the President's spiritual attitude and could serve as a special Reagan credo:

"I know in my heart that man is good, that what is right will always eventually triumph, and there is purpose and worth to each and every life."

In 1981 in a speech for the First Annual Commemoration of the Days of Remembrance for Victims of the Holocaust, he said,

"There is an American poem that says humanity, with all its fears and all its hopes, depends on us. As a matter of fact, it was the Pope, at the end of World War II, when the world was so devastated, and yet, we alone remained so strong, who said: 'America has a genius for great and unselfish deeds, and into the hands of America, God has placed an afflicted mankind.' "

The degree to which Reagan suffered adversity inwardly in his adult life is scarcely known by anyone. We do know that he was devastated by his unexpected divorce from his first wife, the actress Jane Wyman; by a declining film career; by defeat in his first attempt at the nomination for President; by challenges in his relationships with his children; by the major adversity of the assassination attempt that brought him close to death; by physical ailments requiring surgery; and by his final disability. But we do not know how he interpreted or processed these apparent sufferings in his own view of life. There is no record that he dwelt on adversity but he most probably overcame it with his well-documented attitude of trust, faith, and overwhelming optimism. Also, because he did not show any particular self-absorption, depression, or extraordinary introspection, it appears that his character was turned more outward—in a resilient way. If he had only publicly revealed more on this subject, we would be able to fill in the gaps more easily. On the other hand, if he had, he might not have been perceived as a strong, uncomplicated leader. He did not complain or seek sympathy to win support. He didn't need it.

His tendency was to see adversity and its uses on a global or macro scale, rather than a strictly personal one, and also as a part of God's design for reformation. He also linked adversity to optimism, because he did not think man should be conquered by trouble but rather use trouble to improve and cast off any type of bondage from exterior forces. Also, he did not link adversity to finality or to death. He believed that man could always improve his situation. You could see that in the way he looked into the eyes of the collectivist farmers we visited one day in China in 1984. He didn't exactly pity them, but he did provide them with the feeling that there was a better way, a better economic ideal that could be reached. He saw adversity as both a religious problem and a political one, and he saw the solutions in the same way—with his beliefs providing the underpinning and ultimate solution to the problem at hand. He was quietly assessing or judging his life according to what he thought God wanted him to do all along the way, although he would have—wisely—thought it inappropriate to burden anyone else with this self-assessment.

The seasoned but perpetual sunny optimism that was a noticeable element in Reagan's character was not mere intellectual immaturity or political puffery. He believed that his attitude of hope and enthusiasm could actually help turn economies around, affect the stock market, boost public confidence and spending habits, and generally lift confidence in ways that result in moving a country forward. For Reagan, life was not a roll of the dice or a series of lucky deals. It was his belief that God ultimately held the universe in His hands and that the outcome would be good. He shared that belief in almost every speech he gave.

Reagan had a unique opportunity during his presidency, because of the timing of changing events in the Soviet Union and its leadership, which he made use of. He had earned the right to lead a nation founded on the rejection of religious domination and persecution and on the establishment of an environment of toleration and the protection of an individual's right to worship or not in whatever way desired. Reagan's private faith took on a public, global purpose, and he had the opportunity to express it in a way that few people ever have. He did not espouse any specific religious sect, organization, or teaching separate from adherence to the Scriptures.

The Founding Fathers also represented religious plurality and various faith traditions. Jefferson removed selections from the Bible that he believed in and created his own collection of Scriptural writings, now called the Jefferson Bible. For Reagan it was never about sect. His faith was based on a personal relationship with his God, and he called on God as an active presence in his life. I believe he lived a postdenominational life before it was fashionable to state it that way.

Reagan was largely ecumenical and had a healthy respect for Catholics and Jews especially, but he also did not rule out, limit, or criticize any denomination. Our White House staff included persons of many different religions. At an Ecumenical Prayer Breakfast in Dallas in 1984, Reagan said,

"I believe that faith and religion play a critical role in the political life of our nation—and always have—and that the church, and by that I mean all churches, all denominations, has had a strong influence on the state. And this has worked to our benefit as a nation. Those who created our country, the Founding Fathers and Mothers, understood that there

is a divine order which transcends the human order. They saw the state, in fact, as a form of moral order and felt that the bedrock of moral order is religion."

While ecumenical, Reagan was not a bland or passive religionist, nor did he compartmentalize his faith into a convenient, cloistered part of his life or career. He respected and upheld the importance of the constitutional separation of church and state; however, he never separated himself as President from the divine purpose he saw for his country. The carrying out of this purpose, he felt, was not the province of any particular church or government but rested in the minds and hearts of men and women. That was precisely why, in his view, people needed to be free—free to worship, live, act, create, progress, as they themselves determined.

It brings to mind my own favorite saying of Jefferson, carved in the entablature of the glistening white rotunda memorial to him on the Tidal Basin in Washington, DC, surrounded by the famous cherry trees: "I have sworn upon the altar of God eternal hostility against every form of tyranny over the mind of man." I believe that Reagan, in pursuing what he felt were man's God-given rights to freedom from tyranny, was on his own crusade to carry out Jefferson's call.

Reagan's faith was put to the ultimate test when he assumed the highest office in America, and when he stepped over the threshold, he did not leave his faith behind; he pressed it into greater service. As we have seen, he used it to reason about domestic and foreign policy and in personal matters. Only a few people ever have an opportunity to apply their faith in this way and make it work for them in the highest governmental or private sector offices. Perhaps that is why the Bible admonishes its readers to pray for heads of state and other leaders. In the case of Reagan, he returned the favor.

In Reagan's mind, faith was woven into every aspect of his life, and he expressed it in deeply moving terms but typically only when applied to the situations, events, tragedies, and policy objectives he navigated as President. He did not evangelize for religious purposes. He also did not generally associate his faith and walk with any sectarian or stridently religiopolitical issues, organizations, rallies, or political action. It wasn't that he was stopped by his staff from doing so; he wasn't inclined to. More often than not, he also had the good sense to speak in other people's voices—quoting extensively from and referring to the well-recognized, broadly respected leaders of the past. He would tell stories of everyday heroic people whose lives gave inspiration to him and were models for him to talk about. In fact he did this so effectively that people were often surprised to learn of the depth of his own faith.

While I have called Reagan an evangelist for conservative ideals and ideas, he did not attempt to convert or to prejudice another's point of view; instead, he laid out the options. He did not force his voice into anyone's home, but he was grateful to be welcomed there. He carried the banner for conservatism and the Republican Party, but his standard represented far more than that. Reagan publicly professed his faith on numerous occasions.

Beyond that he did not talk about it informally and personally, and yet he expressed it in every single speech he gave. Reagan had an uncanny sense that a personal expression of this faith would not accrue to his popularity or his general overall acceptance as a leader, and might marginalize some of his constituents and color his actions, especially in regard to his foreign policy initiatives. He was aware that he was President for all Americans, not just the devoted. For a period after Reagan's death it continued to surprise me that so few people grasped the depth of his faith or knew anything about it. In retrospect, I now believe that was a fortuitous phenomenon, aiding him in the work he had to do and embellishing his stature in history unassociated with much but his specific accomplishments. I believe that was his intent.

CHAPTER EIGHT

Looking Evil in the Eye

Here is how Natan Sharansky, the Russian Jew who was imprisoned for thirteen years in Soviet work camps, mostly in solitary confinement in Perm35, located in Siberia, dramatically explained the way Reagan's 1983 "Evil Empire" speech reached him. He described it after his release in a deal brokered between Reagan and Gorbachev in 1986.

The story went like this: The words in Reagan's speech were actually spread through the Soviet work camp by primitive Morse code, a long-abandoned wireless dot-and-dash system used in World War I. These words of Reagan were then written out in longhand on small pieces of paper and the papers taped to the walls of Sharansky's gulag, where he had been sentenced as a criminal for, among other things, starting the Refusenik group in Moscow years earlier. There all the prisoners could see and read the words spoken by the American President and pin their hopes on words of someone a world away who was calling out the system under which they were incarcerated. Of this miraculous transmission of the speech, Sharansky wrote, "Finally the leader of the free world had spoken the truth—a truth that burned inside the heart of each and every one of us."

Reagan's remarks and the tireless work of Sharansky's wife and others to win his release ultimately gained Sharansky his freedom in an exchange of prisoners by Mikhail Gorbachev. Sharansky went on to be awarded the United States Medal of Freedom, which was bestowed on him in the East Room of the White House in recognition of his persistent efforts to promote freedom around the world.

Most people try to avoid thinking and talking about evil, hoping it will just go away or somehow be defeated without direct and costly effort. Reagan obviously felt the opposite. To him, identifying evil and talking about it *would* help to make it go away. In this highly noticed March 1983 Orlando speech to the National Association of Evangelicals, Reagan called out the Soviet Union as *"the focus of evil in the modern world."* He also referred to the Soviet Union as an *"evil empire."*

He did not apply these inflammatory labels unknowingly. Reagan was pointed and deliberate when he used these phrases for strategic impact. This was not a stab in the dark for the unequivocal Reagan, although the question remains: What did he mean by these terms? After all, evil is a big subject that perplexes and overwhelms even theologians.

In the cases where Reagan used the term *evil*, he was using it to describe the power of tyrants to deprive the people whom they controlled of free will, which Reagan saw as a natural right of every human being. The oppression of the individual—by a government or dictator—is what he was calling evil in this case. On a basic level, few people could disagree with Reagan. Many felt, however, that it was not appropriate nor timely for him to state it publicly in such a candid, direct, and unmasked way. Their reaction was partly political and partly based on their ignorance of evil's propensities, uses, and potential results—and on the fact that they were not comfortable confronting it, especially when it appeared in another sovereign country.

In particular, Reagan's opponents in the U.S. government thought calling the Soviet system evil would not help our bilateral relationship with the USSR just when these U.S. officials thought we might be on the edge of a thaw. But Reagan knew that evil and evil perpetrators like nothing better than to be left alone to conduct their misdeeds. He also felt that if they were left alone, they would carry out greater crimes that could eventually and directly threaten the security of the United States. Reagan felt that these instigators of evil and wrongdoing had already been at work long enough, and he was ready to provide the world with a wake-up call and label the Soviet system as he saw it.

Prior to World War II, still bearing the memory and the human and economic cost of World War I, much of Europe tried appeasement as a strategy with Hitler until they realized, almost too late, the massive price of that inaction, ignorance, tolerance, and weakness. They had failed to recognize evil, despite ample evidence that it was on the march, and they failed to mount sufficient resistance to it. This was a moral failing and not just a political one. Since Reagan was as much the moral man as he was the politician, it would not even occur to him to treat evil passively. This was Reagan's underlying philosophy, as supported by the details in his many speeches and policy direction.

I believe that Reagan saw evil in both a Biblical archetype and also in an active and practical political framework—and this was a perfect blend for him. He was a Bible student who occupied a secular, political job. He was no moral relativist.

He saw everything as either good or bad. He believed in absolute truth. What was especially interesting to me was that since Reagan was a self-described and hopeless optimist, I would have expected him to take a path of avoidance when it came to evil, preferring to see everything in a positive light—after all, Reagan held a lifelong attitude that everything would turn out all right. But Reagan was ready to do battle with evil, whereas most people take a detour when it comes to facing down a powerful force of wrongdoing. His courageous confrontation with evil deserves respect, and this may have been his strongest contribution as an American leader—the strongest example he could have set—though it is perhaps the least understood feature of his legacy as President.

Reagan saw this arm wrestling with evil systems as a struggle that he was willing to undertake, and he was willing to accept the significant amount of criticism to which he was subjected as a result. His conviction and his courage enabled him to go to battle over the evil of communism and to help stop what it was attempting—which was, at one point in history, a publicly stated goal of world domination, a coming attraction of what we see in today's struggle with radical Islam. In Reagan's advance toward evil, there was in what he said just a headlights-on approach. It is important to note, though, that he was not arguing or pleading for anything. He was stating the facts and building a case for other people to see evil as he did.

Reagan denounced evil in macro terms but did not denounce people who exemplified the very evil he excoriated. It was the systems and uses of evil he was targeting. He wanted to destroy the root causes and strike a final deathblow on it, not just take out the temporary promoters of it. When he talked about the *"ash heap of history"* in describing the end of communism, I believe he imagined the final end to evil systems, not just to its current actors.

This is interesting in comparison to succeeding administrations and their labeling of evil. George W. Bush referred to the "axis of evil," which was somewhat effective but became more personal when he was pressed to name specific evil perpetrators—which he did. Reagan's evil was not personal, not limited to individual politicians but to the teaching and practice of tyranny in political systems and dynasties. He was also willing to accede to redemption. When asked during his visit to Moscow in 1988 if the "evil empire was no longer evil," he admitted that was correct, owing to its significant reforms—thus proving that he saw evil impersonally.

The Outcome of Directly Facing Evil

Though in the United States the "Evil Empire" speech was reviled by liberals who soundly denounced it in the most scathing terms, the reaction of those who were better acquainted with and lived under totalitarian regimes was quite the opposite. That was all that mattered, because Reagan was speaking for them and to them. Paul Kengor has done a masterful job of providing a comprehensive inventory of what happened in the wake of this denunciation. Quoting Sergei Tarasenko of the Soviet Foreign Ministry itself, Kengor reported him saying, "Okay. Well, we are an evil empire." Kengor's report continues with a well-known senior Soviet arms negotiator: " 'You know what caused the downfall of the Soviet Union? You know what did it?' he thundered, slamming his fist on the table. 'That damned speech about the evil empire! That's what did it . . . It *was* an evil empire. It was!' " And then from Arkady Murashev, the Moscow Police Chief who told the *Washington Post* that Reagan "called [the USSR] the 'Evil Empire.' So why did you in the West laugh at him? It's true!" And finally Kengor quotes the former U.S. Ambassador to the USSR, Jack Matlock, as saying that "while this offended the Soviet rulers at the time, it did much to undermine the claim to legitimacy of the Soviet empire."

I would add that it did much to undermine the legitimacy of any or all evil—to call it out—to call its bluff by exposing it and denouncing it. This was the first step, but the most important one, in defeating it. Reagan did not give up his haranguing and pestering and drumbeat of outrage until the breakdown of the communist bloc was complete.

Negotiating with the Soviets on behalf of the White House, I could see that they lived and promoted the propagandistic "big lie" theory, stating and restating it for so many years that millions who lived in tyranny actually came to believe it—or at least tolerate it with the few options left open to them to protest it. When we began our negotiations with the Soviets in planning the Geneva Summit, Gorbachev had been on the job only a relatively short period of time, and his top lieutenants were holdovers from Konstantin Chernenko, his immediate predecessor. Everything we requested in terms of the outline, substance, agenda, structure, and protocol for upcoming meetings was rejected out of hand with an air of decided superiority. Our Soviet counterparts used every opportunity to press the big lie on us that the Soviet system was the biggest and most successful economy in the world and that its citizens enjoyed the greatest freedoms and the finest quality of life.

Listening to these declarations day after day made the fact that these were lies even more obvious. After all, several of us had actually traveled to the USSR and observed the living conditions of its people with our own eyes. On my own visits, I had been stalked and trailed by the KGB and yet was able to talk with ordinary citizens who were quietly candid with me about their extremely poor living conditions and repression. At the negotiating table we talked among ourselves, wondering how smart people such as these government officials could be made to believe these lies. We assumed many knew the truth in their hearts, but that they had few opportunities to demand anything that would threaten their safe and comfortable government positions.

As we prepared for the first Reagan-Gorbachev summit in Geneva, we were not impressed by these lies. But after repeated meetings, we struggled to make any progress in our negotiations because of their line of reasoning based on these lies. As the time grew closer for the meeting between these two superpower leaders, Gorbachev's influence at the negotiating table finally came into play through the appointment of his own staff of political appointees. As a result the names and faces at the bargaining table changed dramatically overnight. The Gorbachev negotiators took on a new tone, which was more mature, honest, candid, and sophisticated. There was a general feeling on our team that these were people we could work with and that perhaps this would foreshadow the tone of the President's experience with Gorbachev at his first of four historic summit meetings with the Soviet leader. Finally everything about this meeting seemed right in terms of timing and content.

The world had paid a steep price for the long Cold War—perhaps not in the dramatic number of casualties that could have occurred if it had been fought militarily, but in the loss of economic growth, the loss of human potential on the world scene, and the terror and fear millions felt on all sides. The economic strain of a massive defensive military buildup and deployment was significant for many countries. Reagan knew that his was a war of ideals and felt he could win the hearts and minds of a majority of any people living in tyranny by calling out a lie, as well as engineering many other complex military, diplomatic, trade, and cultural initiatives—all of which were pieces of his mosaic.

At a much earlier period in his life, Reagan had watched movies of Nazi concentration camps being liberated. He was so impressed with this documented evidence and so repulsed by what the perpetrators had done that he kept the footage and made sure that each of his children saw it. His son Ron Jr. said, "Dad seemed to regard watching that film as an essential rite of manhood."

What was especially useful and timely for the world in Reagan's philosophy and his action as a leader, was his awareness of evil and his political daring to help put an end to its domination in the modern world—at least in its embodiment in the communist rule led by the Soviet Union. Reagan sometimes rejected the advice of high-minded and well-educated advisors in his own government but was joined in his campaign most notably by Pope John Paul II and by Margaret Thatcher, among other players on the field.

While the President was calling out the evil empire, he was also planning for its eventual demise and a strengthening of bilateral relations. We on the staff were planning the details of the first bilateral meeting between Reagan and Gorbachev on the shores of Lake Geneva in late 1985, as Reagan was choreographing a private one-on-one meeting for himself with Gorbachev. This was the way the President would gauge the character of the Soviet leader.

This private, leaders-only session had its roots in a series of briefings Reagan had received in Washington from Suzanne Massie. She had acquired special knowledge of the current state of thinking in the Soviet Union through her many years of travel there, meeting with the Russian people, and writing about them. To his surprise Reagan did not find all of Massie's views represented in his State Department briefing books, and out of curiosity he began meeting with her off the record. Eventually they had dozens of in-person discussions over a period of four years in the White House. The President found her insights especially interesting and useful as they related to the texture of the Russian people, their religion and culture, as well as their leaders' personalities.

Massie also posited that Gorbachev was a man of values and beliefs who might not have been an atheist, although his wife surely was. This gave Reagan his opening with Gorbachev. It was the key he needed, he thought, to create a bridge of understanding. Gorbachev was someone he felt he could work with, and this proved to be true. He carried Massie's many insights with him to Geneva along with his State Department briefings.

In Geneva, the Reagans stayed in the handsome but moderate-sized villa of the Aga Khan, the spiritual leader of a sect of Shia Muslims. Nancy Reagan had personally approved the selection of this house after our team had spent days scouting and touring many possible sites in and around Geneva. Most of the formal meetings took place at the larger, more businesslike Villa Fleur d'Eau a short distance from where the Reagans were housed. This venue had room for some media and staff. It also had a small rustic cottage, which some called a pool house, by Lake Geneva, a hundred yards or so from the main building. The cottage had a large fireplace, and it was here that the first separate and exclusive meeting took place— just the two men and their interpreters. Just the way Reagan wanted it. Here the leaders were away from staff and other formalities so Reagan could carry out his one simple purpose: Establish an understanding between them based upon the possibility of a shared belief in a Higher Power. This was Reagan's idea alone.

There was skepticism among the staff about whether or not this was a wise idea, and there was opposition to the two leaders being alone without staff or note takers, only interpreters. Some could see danger in it. Reagan felt it was worth the risk to establish a personal relationship based on some level of possible emerging trust. He would often say that he had waited a long time to meet with a Soviet leader, as several of Gorbachev's predecessors had died in office after serving only a short time, and this was the first meeting between the heads of the two superpowers in six years.

Here was Reagan's chance to put his belief system to use in a high-stakes gamble to establish a positive working relationship. The world was watching. Reagan was performing in textbook fashion. He was attempting to establish a basis for communication with Gorbachev in laying the groundwork for subsequent meetings that would bring the two into conflict on a host of serious issues. If it was not complete mutual trust that resulted from these private meetings, it was at least honesty and candor. On Reagan's part his goal was to achieve a sufficient level of understanding between the two leaders that they could move forward to address the issues of highest importance to the world. The stakes were high in terms of potential global impact, and both men knew that.

I remember vividly the early evening hours before Gorbachev's arrival for dinner at the Reagans' compound. There was a somewhat unsurprising pensive atmosphere in the house while the outside world watched to see how these leaders would relate and what, if anything, they would accomplish. I had asked the Aga Khan if he would be willing to leave some of his personal staff, including his own chef, to help run the house during our stay. He kindly agreed to my request. That day they had built a roaring fire in a massive stone fireplace in the center of the main salon or living room, with its comfortable red-damask-upholstered furniture.

While waiting for Gorbachev, Reagan and I sat alone for some time in front of the fire, relaxing and mostly sharing small talk about the trip. I turned to him at one point and asked a more probing question.

"What," I asked him plainly, "in your own personal view will ultimately send totalitarian and communist regimes, the systems you call evil, to what you often call the ash heap of history once and for all—and when will the conflict with the Soviet Union finally be resolved?" I really wanted to know if he had any real insight as to when these "failed experiments in government," as he characterized them, would fall and how.

"Jim," he said in that quiet and low baritone, *"these systems will crumble by the sheer fact that a growing majority of people living under their rule have a pent-up desire to be free to worship more than the state; and this demand to know and worship God, and to have a free and open relationship with Him, is what will bring totalitarianism and communism down. Of this I am sure. The people will do it themselves. We need to do everything we can to help them accomplish this."*

This was obviously a variation on one of the principal underlying themes he was pursuing in the one-on-one meetings with the Soviet President, and much of this thinking had come from his discussions with Suzanne Massie as well as his own reservoir of beliefs. But it was also pure Reagan to think longitudinally and contrary to publicly disclosed strategy that had focused necessarily and appropriately on a U.S. military buildup and its resulting economic pressure on the Soviet system. Alternatively he could have heard what Massie had to report about the Russian people and their deeply felt religious beliefs and disregarded it. Instead he decided to act on it. After hearing him predict the future in the way he did for me in front of the fire, I had little doubt that Reagan connected his personal beliefs to his policy and statecraft. I believe he saw himself in a larger battle that he hoped would end in a victory for democracy and freedom.

I took what Reagan had said to heart, thought about it over and over again, and rarely repeated it to anyone. Had his answer to my question been leaked to the media, it would have been soundly discredited, and had it been repeated to policy makers who were correctly and honestly pursuing a two-front, aggressive military and diplomatic strategy, it would also have been dismissed. But what could not be dismissed was that the belief that Reagan held and shared with me was eventually verified by history—by what actually took place. The churches in Eastern Europe did play a significant role in the demise of totalitarianism in a way that could not have been politically engineered or even imagined at the time of the November 1985 summit.

Anne Applebaum, the Pulitzer Prize–winning journalist, sheds light on what was then happening in Eastern Europe to confirm Reagan's perceptions. She has explained the work of Pope John Paul II and the churches in Poland in the creation of Solidarity, the first union organized to defeat communism. These were the efforts to ultimately organize civil society in a way that would play a significant role in the defeat of the Soviet Union. In a 2005 *Washington Post* article entitled "How the Pope 'Defeated Communism,'" she wrote:

"My husband, 16 years old at the time, remembers climbing a tree on the outskirts of an airfield near Gniezno where the pope was saying Mass and seeing an endless crowd 'three kilometers in every direction.' The regime—its leaders, its police—were nowhere visible: 'There were so many of us, and so few of them.' That was also the trip in which the pope kept repeating, 'Don't be afraid.'

"It wasn't a coincidence that the Poles found the courage, a year later, to organize Solidarity...It wasn't a coincidence that 'civil society' began to organize itself in other communist countries as well: If it could happen in Poland, it could happen in Hungary or East Germany...Nor was it necessary, in 1989, for the pope to do deals with Gorbachev, since in 1979 he had already demonstrated the hollowness of the Soviet Union's claims to moral superiority. He didn't need to conduct secret negotiations, because he'd already shown that the most important things could be said in public. He didn't need to man the barricades, in other words, because he had already shown people that they could walk right through them."

In Reagan's signature achievement of helping to end the Cold War and the communist rule and policy of global expansionism, we see a leader who is searching for the ending and he finds it, not surprisingly, in something that is attuned to his own beliefs. The end of any story for Reagan has to be based in faith and truth—as he spoke about in direct terms and is in evidence everywhere in his speeches. I believe that Reagan saw the world not solely in the history of material achievements and human strife but in phases of human progress, its trajectory sometimes arrested by tyrants but always on a forward, if not a visibly apparent, ascent. Though he was ridiculed for holding this perspective, it separated Reagan from the political pack. It gave him a stature that most were not able to precisely define and about which Reagan did not help to make plain.

CHAPTER NINE

Chief Salesman

Reagan was always selling. In fact, Mike Deaver, his closest aide, always said Reagan would have made a great shoe salesman. But as President, just like a purveyor of footwear, he also had to have a quality product to sell. In 1980, by the time of Reagan's inauguration, he had told the American people repeatedly what he would do if he were elected President. This was the product he sold them: a platform of positions, policies, and initiatives he would undertake for the country—all with the underpinning of his unique conservative belief system.

However, as soon as he unpacked his bags at 1600 Pennsylvania Avenue, he had to start all over again, just as every newly elected President does, and restate to the public and important members of Congress the details of his political platform. For the voters with whom he entered a new type of relationship, he was no longer candidate Reagan but the chief executive. That meant a whole new round of scrutiny of the man and learning the way he would govern.

His initial selling job was interrupted by the assassination attempt a little more than two months into his first term. But this unexpected and unimaginable incident also provided an unplanned sympathetic lift to his legislative agenda and strengthened both his resolve and his ability to sell it. With Reagan the salesman, everything was symbolic as well as practical, and his appearance before an unusual joint session of Congress twenty-nine days after the shooting was designed to regain the upper hand of the presidency through the symbolism of a healthy body (his) and the productive relationship he sought with a healthy body politic (the Congress).

When he strode into the House chamber on April 28, 1981, and finally began his speech, after ten minutes of sustained applause and very few dry eyes, on either side of the aisle, his survival had a special meaning to these legislators and in some way united them. At that moment Reagan was not a partisan. He was just an American—as were they. Reagan began his address by thanking his fellow Americans for their support, prayers, and love during his recuperation, but he lost no time getting to the heart of his plan. He renewed his call for Congress to pass his agenda, which included tax reform and cuts, curbs on federal spending, and a stimulus for the economy.

From the time in 1962 when he turned to the right politically and became a Republican, Reagan always had to justify his views, run a little harder, explain a little more, and sell more ambitiously than when he was a card-carrying Democrat. You could say that the full debut of Reagan's platform and program, which he would begin to sell as President in 1981, had a much earlier unveiling in Phoenix at the 1964 Republican National Convention, when Barry Goldwater was nominated for President. It was Reagan's first major exposure as a politician on the national scene, and he made a big impression with his electrifying "Time for Choosing" speech (or "Rendezvous with Destiny," as it was also dubbed).

In his youth, Reagan was a well-paid lifeguard on the Rock River, where he was credited with saving seventy-seven lives. In fact, he always saw himself as a "lifeguard" throughout his varied careers.

Reagan was the son of a preacher—his mother, Nelle. She instilled in him an understanding of God that became his permanent point of reference.

Reagan tried out his political beliefs in speeches he wrote by hand on yellow-lined pads and delivered at the GE factory gates and in his role as a corporate spokesman.

Reagan reviews a policy paper on Private Sector Initiatives (PSI) as we walk from the Oval Office with Vice President Bush.

Fresh from delivering the kick-off speech for his favorite domestic policy program, PSI.

The Reagans in Berlin, where the President spoke six of the most iconic words of the twentieth century: *"Mr. Gorbachev, tear down this wall!"*

The Reagans never liked being away from each other for more than a night or two. Here we are returning from Nancy Reagan's solo meeting with the Pope at the Vatican. She is reuniting with the President during his state visit in Germany.

A fateful, gray day that included a controversial eight-minute stop at a cemetery in Bitburg, Germany, where Nazi SS soldiers were buried. The visit created a small firestorm of controversy.

The start of bridge building with Gorbachev.

The Reagans hosted Gorbachev and his wife, Raisa, for dinner at the first summit between the two leaders.

THE WHITE HOUSE
WASHINGTON

Dear Claire
Thank you very
much for my card. You
were very nice to think of
me & I'm grateful.
I love you too.
Sincerely
Ronald Reagan

The handwritten note to my five-year-old daughter that Reagan penned from his hospital bed. *"Dear Claire, Thank you very much for my card. You were very nice to think of me and I'm grateful. I love you too. Sincerely, Ronald Reagan."*

In the Blue Room of the White House after having returned from Bethesda Naval Hospital, where Reagan underwent cancer surgery. He is wearing the outfit he had asked me to pick out for him from his White House closet.

Reagan visits the demilitarized zone between North and South Korea during a state visit.

Returning to the United States from a trip to Seoul, South Korea, with two young children who required heart surgery in the United States.

Dancing to gospel music at a local Washington, DC, inner-city church.

Cutting loose on Air Force One after a state visit in Europe.

Visiting the First
Emperor's Terracotta
Warriors in Xi'an,
China.

We are all tired,
including the
President, after a
long-haul flight
on Air Force One,
returning from a
state visit abroad.

In England catching
up with Reagan's close
friend and ally Margaret
Thatcher after a three-day
trip to Ireland, the land of
Reagan's ancestors.

Reagan delivering the famous Guildhall speech in London, England.

Queen Elizabeth and Prince Philip visit Rancho del Cielo and the small adobe ranch house that Reagan built with his own hands. This was during the soggy five-day trip that the British monarch made to California.

Reagan visits Omaha Beach for the fortieth anniversary of the Allied landing in Normandy. He circulates with Queen Elizabeth of the United Kingdom, President Mitterrand of France, and Queen Beatrix of the Netherlands, who can be seen in the blue hat and dark coat.

We thought dogs were the answer to a White House without children! Here the first Reagan dog, a Bouvier des Flandres named Lucky, takes control of the President's helicopter, Marine One, en route to Camp David.

We wait at the front door of the White House for the formal state arrival of the Sultan of Brunei.

Briefing Reagan in the family quarters. It looks like I am scolding him, so the President wrote on the photo, *"Dear Jim—OK, I won't do it again. Best regards, Ronald Reagan."*

The Reagans always carefully familiarized themselves with and followed the script during the program for any event.

A part of every state visit for a foreign head of state included formal military honors. Reagan loved every minute of it. Here President and Mrs. Marcos of the Philippines are welcomed.

Waiting in the glare of the White House press pool with the Reagans for an arriving guest at the north entrance.

With the President at one of the annual Congressional Picnics on the South Lawn of the White House. He wrote to me on this photo, *"Dear Jim—See, the White House can be fun if you dress for it. Best Regards, Ronald Reagan."*

In the Blue Room of the White House.

Special Olympians give the President bear hugs on the South Lawn of the White House while wary Secret Service agents stand by.

Mother Teresa meeting with the Reagans in the White House.

Chatting with my wife, Nancy. The President inscribed the photo, *"Dear Nancy and Jim—It really is a pleasure. Warmest regards, Ronald Reagan."*

After a televised Oval Office speech, Reagan is congratulated by daughter Maureen Reagan and her husband, Dennis Revell.

The Reagans celebrating their anniversary at lunch in the office—the Oval Office.

The man at his ranch. He said, *"There is nothing so good for the mind of a man than the back of a horse."*

Reagan called this Arnold Friberg painting of George Washington "sublime" and saw it as an idealistic image of a strong American leader. (For more information on Arnold Friberg's artwork, please visit www.fribergfineart.com.)

After that, he never looked back, never gave up selling his principles and beliefs, until he was in effect silenced by the degrading disease and disability that took his voice. In this speech, delivered in Goldwater's home town of Phoenix, Arizona, the expectations for Reagan's performance were not high, to say the least, and there were questions about why he was even selected to give this key endorsement. But this was an ideal situation for him to be in at that convention.

Reagan would frequently remind us on the staff of this precept—to always surprise an audience with greatness, and this became a sort of mantra in the West Wing. Do not promise anything before you can deliver it. Do not preempt yourself with immodesty. Do not overpromise in quantity or quality. Go in to the audience with lower expectations and come out surprising them with an impressive achievement so that they sit up and take notice, where they had expected not to be moved or impressed, or even to remember anything you said or did. This attitude, practiced by Reagan, sometimes even in an "aw shucks" manner, put him in a position to say, in part, at that national debut speech in Phoenix:

"You and I know and do not believe that life is so dear and peace so sweet as to be purchased at the price of chains and slavery. If nothing in life is worth dying for, when did this begin—just in the face of this enemy? Or should Moses have told the children of Israel to live in slavery under the pharaohs? Should Christ have refused the cross? Should the patriots at Concord Bridge have thrown down their guns and refused to fire the shot heard 'round the world? The martyrs of history were not fools, and our honored dead who gave their lives to stop the advance of the Nazis didn't die in vain. Where, then, is the road to peace? Well it's a simple answer after all.

"You and I have the courage to say to our enemies, 'There is a

*price we will not pay.' 'There is a point beyond which they must not
advance.' And this—this is the meaning in the phrase of Barry Goldwater's 'peace through strength.' Winston Churchill said, 'The destiny
of man is not measured by material computations. When great forces
are on the move in the world, we learn we're spirits, not animals.' And
he said, 'There's something going on in time and space, and beyond time
and space, which, whether we like it or not, spells duty. You and I have
a rendezvous with destiny."*

The interesting thing about this speech is not the effect it
had on the Goldwater campaign—$1 million came pouring in
the very night of the speech. Nor was it the effect on Reagan's
political prospects—which advanced rapidly from this point.
It was that this speech provides evidence Reagan was talking,
selling, and sermonizing to huge crowds long before he had a
stable of speechwriters in the White House. This is definitive
proof that his public speaking skills as President did not accrue
principally to the extraordinary skill of brilliant speechwriters
but to Reagan himself. Reagan wrote these things, this entire
speech, himself from a boyhood of learning from sermons, a
profession of talking to millions on the radio, acting on the big
screen, and by imagining the possible and describing what he
understood as a nation's destiny.

Few men or women ever have the opportunity or courage to say the things Reagan did to such extraordinarily large
audiences. He was never called a preacher's son publicly, and I
am not sure why, because he was. He was Nelle Reagan's son.
Preachers have something to sell—be it fire and brimstone, the
Ten Commandments, the Sermon on the Mount, or redemption and restoration. Reagan was patterning himself and his
leadership style on this—the selling leadership style of the
church. The only difference was that the platform was secu-

lar and the results were open to anyone. Reagan, as national political leader, had to sell the redemption of a governmental system he thought to be broken, and he had to sell military rearmament, a regaining of American power and stature in the world, and a long list of domestic policy proposals.

Because Reagan was elected President on a platform that included tax relief and economic reform and he had innovative ideas about how to achieve them, he was frequently put in a position of explaining and proving his big ideas—and then having to defend the details before he could roll them out more broadly and sell them to the public. This was how he described the situation he found in Washington a month after he took office:

"A few days ago I was presented with a report I'd asked for, a comprehensive audit, if you will, of our economic condition. You won't like it. I didn't like it. But we have to face the truth and then go to work to turn things around. And make no mistake about it, we can turn them around...

"Regulations adopted by government with the best of intentions have added $666 to the cost of an automobile. It is estimated that altogether regulations of every kind, on shopkeepers, farmers, and major industries, add $100 billion or more to the cost of the goods and services we buy. And then another $20 billion is spent by government handling the paperwork created by those regulations.

"I'm sure you're getting the idea that the audit presented to me found government policies of the last few decades responsible for our economic troubles. We forgot or just overlooked the fact that government—any government—has a built-in tendency to grow. Now, we all had a hand in looking to government for benefits, as if government had some source of revenue other than our earnings."

In this talk, Reagan was laying the groundwork for his sales initiative. He reminded people repeatedly what the situation was like when he arrived in Washington. He was setting the baseline record straight, as he saw it, and drawing a line in the sand against which he would be judged for the actions he took to improve economic conditions. These were the "starting block" statements and the beginning of this big sales push. He had to state plainly his assessment of the situation he inherited in order to make his projections about the future and have them heard. He set a perfect pattern for any salesman to follow: Articulate the conditions on arrival, then lay out the plan to fix them, just as any general called to battle would also do. After this opener, he turned the oratorical corner with a more detailed statement of the problem and then started a turn to the future in these words from his April 1981 speech to Congress:

"It's been a half a year since the election that charged all of us in this government with the task of restoring our economy. And where have we come in these six months? Inflation, as measured by the Consumer Price Index, has continued at a double-digit rate. Mortgage interest rates have averaged almost fifteen percent for these six months, preventing families across America from buying homes. There are still almost eight million unemployed. The average worker's hourly earnings after adjusting for inflation are lower today than they were six months ago, and there have been over 6,000 business failures.

"Six months is long enough! The American people now want us to act, and not in half measures. They demand and they've earned a full and comprehensive effort to clean up our economic mess. Because of the extent of our economy's sickness, we know that the cure will not come quickly and that even with our package, progress will come in inches and feet, not in miles. But to fail to act will delay, even longer and more painfully, the cure which must come. And that cure begins with the federal budget. And the budgetary actions taken by the Congress over

the next few days will determine how we respond to the message of last November 4. That message was very simple: Our government is too big, and it spends too much."

This part of the sales pitch stakes a claim and makes a warning. *"Six months is long enough!"* Change is coming. Get ready for the rest of the story and to take action on the proposals we will make. This is the turn from the statement of the problem to the statement of the solution. Reagan knew what he had to do—as much as if he were the shoe salesman. He restated it from the Oval Office on July 27, 1981, this way:

"In a few days the Congress will stand at the fork of two roads. One road is all too familiar to us. It leads ultimately to higher taxes. It merely brings us full circle back to the source of our economic problems, where the government decided that it knows better than you what should be done with your earnings and, in fact, how you should conduct your life. The other road promises to renew the American spirit. It's a road of hope and opportunity. It places the direction of your life back in your hands where it belongs.

"I've not taken your time this evening merely to ask you to trust me. Instead, I ask you to trust yourselves. That's what America is all about. Our struggle for nationhood, our unrelenting fight for freedom, our very existence—these have all rested on the assurance that you must be free to shape your life as you are best able to, that no one can stop you from reaching higher or take from you the creativity that has made America the envy of mankind. One road is timid and fearful; the other is bold and hopeful."

Finally in this last section he is calling for action, participation from the audience. Reagan was selling his remedy for the idea that America had lost its strong standing in the world. That prospect was intolerable to Reagan, and he knew if he were to be effective on the global scene that had to change.

He put America on notice that he would launch a campaign to spread democracy and freedom wherever he could find a predisposition or a desire for it—and even where he did not.

When he ordered American forces into tiny, nearby Grenada to stop a Marxist coup in Operation Fury in March 1983, he explained his decision to intervene with military force this way, just like any salesman would:

"Grenada, we were told, was a friendly island paradise for tourism. Well, it wasn't. It was a Soviet-Cuban colony, being readied as a major military bastion to export terror and undermine democracy. We got there just in time . . . Sam Rayburn once said that freedom is not something a nation can work for once and win forever. He said it's like an insurance policy; its premiums must be kept up to date. In order to keep it, we have to keep working for it and sacrificing for it, just as long as we live. If we do not, our children may not know the pleasure of working to keep it, for it may not be theirs to keep."

Reagan understood the need for any leader to explain himself, explain his actions and their consequences. This makes the leader stronger and broadens his base of support. This was not only a selling proposition but an educational one for his electorate.

Reagan's 1983 show of force in Grenada was heard throughout the world and noticed as Reagan's willingness to go to war to defend freedom. Action like that, not to occupy but to ferret out and destroy a Marxist cell on the island, helped in a small way to rebuild the strength of America overseas, and it may have helped to bring some reluctant leaders to a more serious place at the bargaining table. This was an example of Reagan's pledge of seeking peace through strength. Successes like the one in Grenada also helped Reagan in selling his next piece of business with the American people.

Reagan came to office with an ambitious and detailed plan, as every President does, that was vetted through the electoral process. Because of his overwhelmingly positive election results, he had a mandate to shift the nation's priorities. As a result, the selling started in earnest at the beginning of his Administration and was an endless rotation of explaining and gaining the ear of the majority who would hear it—and then starting all over again. Selling is like advertising—the key is repetition. Successful political salesmanship is no different. Reagan was repetitive—often to the complaints of journalists who had to record yet another defense of the virtues of limited government and supply-side economics. If he had lost the leading edge of effective salesmanship, he could have lost his considerable political capital.

To expand, solidify, and keep the sales advantage, Reagan took his message directly to the American people. He did this as often as possible in an attempt to influence what might have been the media's own interpretation of his proposals. He didn't want a middleman describing his initiatives. He was confident in his own message, his delivery, and his audience. He did not shortchange them; he respected them. He had the idea that if he could get in front of his audience, physically or virtually, he would have a better chance of convincing them of his sincerity and the value of his proposals. He thought this was the only way to enlist them in an unbiased way and also to move them to take the action he was proposing—the action he was actually *urging* they take. These tactics are reminiscent of the work he did for General Electric in the 1950s, traversing the country talking about and selling management issues at the factory gates—and finding attentive audiences.

Reagan wanted to reason with Americans and show them

why it was important for them to fight to reduce the size and scope of government and to stimulate them to make government their servant rather than their master. Reagan always said, as had Presidents before him, that he had command of the "bully pulpit"—a term coined by President Theodore Roosevelt in reference to the White House and its ability to draw in and compel listeners to hear its message. This bully pulpit was an especially comfortable place for Reagan to occupy because of his natural, son-of-a-preacher training and his predisposition to evangelize on issues important to him and to his political platform. Here is an example of a message to promote his policies, delivered on August 16, 1982:

"There's an old saying we've all heard a thousand times about the weather and how everyone talks about it but no one does anything about it. Well, many of you must be feeling that way about the present state of our economy. Certainly there's a lot of talk about it, but I want you to know we're doing something about it. And the reason I wanted to talk to you is because you can help us do something about it . . .

"I know you've read and heard on the news a variety of statements attributed to various 'authoritative government sources who prefer not to have their names used.' Well, you know my name, and I think I'm an authoritative source on this, since I'm right in the middle of what's going on here. So, I'd like to set the record straight on a few things that you might have heard lately . . . You helped us start this economic recovery program last year when you told your representative you wanted it. You can help again—whether you're a Republican, a Democrat, or an Independent—by letting them know that you want it continued, letting them know that you understand that this legislation is a price worth paying for lower interest rates, economic recovery, and more jobs."

Here Reagan is talking more like a candidate attempting to win votes than a President stating a policy. His tone is eager, his demeanor folksy, his attitude confident and assertive, right out of the once-popular Dale Carnegie book *How to Win Friends and Influence People*. Reagan remained in charge and true to his character, but he was willing to do what it took to win a point or two in public opinion about his programs. This is what it takes for any leader to expand his base of support for an idea, an invention, legislation, a strategy, or a plan—winning points, speech by speech, interview by interview.

He was a "Chairman of the Board" President rather than a "Chief Operating Officer" officeholder. Reagan took a broad stroke in his management style and is remembered less for his specific policies than for his basic beliefs and larger accomplishments. Some chief executives fail to make a clear distinction between management and leadership. Reagan did not. He was not a manager and he knew it. He also knew it required a big-picture thinker, strategist, and leader to earn significant respect and consolidate power, especially in a role like this.

This was precisely what the American people were seeking by rejecting Jimmy Carter for a second term and electing Reagan. Then they sent Reagan back to the White House in 1984 for a second term after he won a landslide victory, taking forty-nine states in his election bid against Democrat Walter Mondale. When voters were asked in exit polls in the 1984 election what they liked most about Reagan, 40 percent said they liked Reagan because he was a "strong leader"; only half that many said they liked any particular position he took. ABC polling director Jeffrey Alderman said at the time that Reagan's early showing of strong leadership in his first term "was enough by itself to buy Reagan the time he needed. It allowed him to survive the worst recession since World War II with much of the public [behind him]."

Selling from the Oval Office

One powerful sales tool uniquely available to any U.S. President is to talk to the American people from the massive antique desk in the Oval Office. From there Ronald Reagan could look them straight in the eye, through the camera lens, without interference or interruption. Reagan set the record for the greatest number of presidential talks televised from the Oval Office. He addressed the nation twenty-nine times from that iconic room, which had been added to the White House complex during the William Howard Taft Administration. It is the most powerful and well-recognized office in the world. Reagan was aware of that and treated it reverentially. These were prime-time major network events that interrupted people's favorite nightly TV shows. The White House received complaints about taking time away from regularly scheduled programs, but millions listened, and many who did valued this chat with their President.

Whether you agreed with what he said or not, the power of the Oval Office talk was undeniable. It was an effective and productive way for him to reach people, and there was a kind of comfort in Reagan's presentation. We made every attempt to associate these particular talks with the most serious issues. I would characterize these talks by Reagan as a very serious discussion you might have had with your dad, grandfather, or mentor, where you gave him the courtesy of listening carefully to what he said. At the same time, Reagan was conscious of not overdoing the number of talks from his office, which could have diminished their importance.

Some Oval Office talks attracted larger audiences than

others—and this depended upon the viewing competition from other television shows in the same time block and also the subject of the presidential talk. The largest audience tuned in for his farewell address on January 19, 1988. Being in the Oval Office a couple of times during these live productions was a big deal, and I observed that Reagan was focused and scripted and came across as the polished actor he was. When he signed off with his signature "God bless America," you had a feeling that he really did want God to bless America. The reason an observer might have felt that way is because Reagan felt it in his heart. He had more respect for his country and for the Oval Office than he did for himself.

Reagan wanted to build up the power, prestige, and stature of the American presidency as an institution itself—not for his own personal benefit, but to enhance respect for the office throughout the world. He wanted this for political purposes and to uphold one of the most solid, successful, and durable institutions of democracy as an example. The Oval Office talks played into that strategy and enhanced it, because they had a worldwide audience as well as the one at home. He felt that the level of regard accorded the office of the U.S. President was a support to what he could accomplish in promoting democracy and freedom around the world. He cared about what would happen to the office once he left, and he wanted it to be in a better place than when he first occupied it. He wanted a powerful presidency, because of what it would enable him to accomplish globally.

Reagan's ability to talk directly to the American people rested on his ability to gain and retain their interest and confidence. Reagan felt this was linked to the esteem his constituents had for the office as much as their approval of him personally. This was a critical point to him, and it was not lost on his treatment of the symbols of the office. So, for example, when Reagan was in the Oval Office working, you had a sense that he felt awed by his temporary job. I do not think we would be able to find a picture of Ronald Reagan with his feet hoisted up on the edge of the extremely rare, intricately carved, and valuable Resolute desk that he used—something several other Presidents had done. He would have considered that crass and symbolically degrading to the office, and that it would contribute to a disrespect of the office and its role in the world. Reagan relished the pomp and circumstance of the office, the marching bands on the South Lawn, the military color guards, the cannon salutes, the choreographed formal arrivals of heads of state. It was all a part of the montage of a strong presidency, a part of the American fabric—a kilowatt in the shining city metaphor.

Kathy Osborne, the President's longtime secretary, told me that Reagan always felt awed by working in the office where so many epic decisions had been made and so much history created and witnessed. He never lost the thrill of walking into the Oval Office or making his daily commute from the family quarters, through the lower cross hall, and out the West Garden Room to the West Wing. The bust of Churchill, and the handsome Western bronze sculptures by celebrated artist Frederic Remington, as well as the historic George Catlin Indian Chief paintings, were all prominent features of Reagan's office and conveyed a feeling of power, order, and respectability.

Selling on the Road

There was a running joke around the White House (and this is probably true of any presidential administration) that whenever we were having a bad news day in Washington, we needed to take the President out to Andrews Air Force Base, hop on Air Force One, and take a trip. Anywhere. Locating a receptive and supportive audience to talk to can do wonders to demonstrate to the rest of the world that there is robust support for your ideas—somewhere. For Reagan this was usually in the heartland of America, where conservative values were more appreciated than on the East Coast.

Following almost every annual State of the Union address or Oval Office talk, trips to key states and localities were planned to have the message delivered directly to the people by the President or by Cabinet-level officials acting as surrogates. These were handled like campaign trips to sell a new platform of ideas or a legislative agenda. Sometimes the President would be accompanied by the Congressman whose district he would visit or by the Governor of the state. This was also an opportunity for small media outlets to capture and distribute the message, and for Reagan again to talk plainly to his fellow countrymen about the specifics of the proposals presented in the usually ambitious, lengthy State of the Union speech or in an Oval Office talk. On trips to speak about tax reform, he reached out to the heartland. First, from Williamsburg, Virginia:

"Two nights ago I unveiled our proposal to revolutionize the Federal tax code. I spoke of the system as it is now, and as we wish it to be. But just for a moment today I want to note how our modern tax system evolved from a modest attempt to raise modest revenues to the behemoth to which we are currently beholden . . . Our Federal tax system is, in short, utterly impossible, utterly unjust, and completely counterproductive . . . It's earned a rebellion, and it's time we rebelled."

Then from Oshkosh, Wisconsin:

"The night before last, television networks were kind enough to give me a few minutes to talk about our system of taxation. I announced our plan to put more resources into the hands of the American people by making our tax code more simple, fair, and efficient and the most sweeping change in our tax laws it would be in more than seventy years. I knew we were on the right track when the high-priced tax attorneys started shedding tears after I spoke. And now that I've come to Main Street, America, and now that I have seen a smile on the face of Oshkosh, I know we said the right thing."

And from Malvern, Pennsylvania:

"For too long our tax code has been a damper on the economy. Steeply rising tax rates punish success, while tangled and needlessly complicated rules of compliance can booby-trap any new enterprise that can't afford high-priced lawyers and tax consultants to protect itself from the tax man. April 15th wasn't so long ago. And I'm sure many still remember that mounting feeling of frustration and resentment as you worked late into the night trying to make sense of the maze of bureaucratic rules and regulations. Nearly half of all Americans threw up their hands in dismay and went to get professional help on their taxes this year. Well, paying someone to figure out how much you owe the government in taxes just adds insult to injury. Don't you think America's had enough?"

In these regional or local talks, Reagan could break down his agenda into digestible and simple messages. Talking directly to people on these road trips did not have to be grand in the way that an Oval Office or State of the Union talk would have to be. It could be smaller and more intimate, and he could be more accessible. It could also embrace issues confronting the local community. It gave Reagan more face time with Americans as well.

An American incumbent President is the head of his own political party, and he needs to focus on expanding and solidifying its base as well as its current or hoped-for majority. The President should leave his party in better shape than he found it. Not all American Presidents have understood this obligation, and many have failed at it. Reagan adhered to this rule, and it was a central part of his strategy to get out of the White House, to talk with Americans directly and also to fund-raise for his party.

I will never forget accompanying Margaret Thatcher on one of her own road trips—during her 1987 reelection bid—when she returned to her constituency, or electoral district, in Finchley, a London suburb. It was an enlightening experience. As magnificent as the Iron Lady had become globally, she still had to face the local voters in a humble school hall in order to secure her reelection and keep her post at Number 10 Downing Street. She had to return in every election cycle to the very place that had given her political breath and the right to lead. They held the key to her future, and while she was larger than life on the world stage, I saw her assume a much more attentive and modest version of herself on the local stump. She had to secure the vote from her constituents, or she would be packing her bags at the Prime Minister's residence.

Reagan, while serving under a different electoral process, nevertheless did not forget what he owed to the people who voted for him and even to those who did not. They were always his boss, and he respected that. Reagan knew he was President for all American citizens. He relished his responsibility to unite and not to divide along partisan lines or special-interest groups. His ability to unite was one of his most prominent attributes. He was aware that this did not mean he would be personally and uniformly liked nor that his political standing would always ride high. For him it meant to bring together a community of citizens who loved and honored their country regardless of politics.

Reagan saw his role as an orchestra leader, setting the pace and the tempo, and selecting the compositions to be played. Beyond that, managing the minutiae and details of a large federal bureaucracy was not something in which he would become deeply involved on a day-to-day basis. He did create the template for what we called "cabinet government" and made ambitious attempts to maintain strong working relationships with his Cabinet secretaries. He was aided in this by a very effective Cabinet office staff headed by my friend Craig Fuller.

After observing this up close, I had to admit that there is actually no overall Chief Operating Officer for the vast U.S. Government as a singular entity. Any President is held accountable for developments in the U.S. government during his time in office, but he is rarely involved directly in its operations. Cabinet officials and agency heads become the closest to acting like Governors of the states with responsibility for their own territories or agencies. The Director of the Office of Management and Budget position comes closest to assuming the Chief Operating Officer role.

Reagan's "Chairman of the Board" leadership style was put on full display at the annual staff gathering, held at the massive DAR Auditorium a few blocks' walking distance from the White House. Reagan, like any President, had an opportunity to personally appoint approximately 2,500 government employees to carry out his platform and policies, and this gathering was always an impressive collection of Reaganites—as we were called. Every year there was a unique theme to the meeting, which included talks by Cabinet officials and was capped by the President's address itself. I always found these events well-intentioned and effective ways to assemble, unify, and energize a large group of employees. Reagan was in his element at these "family" gatherings. It also provided all these political appointees an ability to return to their individual agencies and share the President's message with all federal employees.

Although Reagan was willing to and did compromise when needed, especially on his legislative agenda, he had a highly developed intuitive sense that he was right on most issues. Whenever I was briefing him, he looked me directly in the eye and he listened intently. You could see the wheels turning. If he agreed with you, he just took your advice and followed what you suggested or outlined. If he did not, he would review his options, usually at a later time.

I remember the contrast between Ronald Reagan and George H. W. Bush in personal briefings. Bush, for whom I also had enormous respect, wanted to be more engaged, was less formal, and would provide feedback on whether or not he agreed with what you were telling him right on the spot, and then he would proceed according to the way *he* thought best. Reagan would usually proceed along the lines that *you* thought were best at least for tactical matters. Reagan was the type of leader who hired the best people to work for him and then expected them to perform to their highest capacity. You did not want to disappoint him, and most did not. His backup was a sophisticated personnel office and a highly focused political operation that thoroughly vetted every appointee for their commitment to conservative values and practices.

I learned about this process firsthand when I ran into the buzz saw of an unyielding political clearance process myself.

I remember, after having already joined the staff, being asked to meet with Lyn Nofziger, the President's longtime political advisor, and told I did not pass the political litmus test. As a lifelong Republican from a Republican family and as an ardent supporter of Reagan, I was both curious and piqued. When I asked him to explain his complaint in detail, I discovered that he had mistakenly associated me with having worked for a well-known liberal. I laughed out loud with relief while explaining to him his error. He had linked me with someone I had never met but who had the same name as my previous boss—who was in fact a stalwart conservative. That matter was cleared up and the subject closed, but I learned a lesson in the degree of political vetting the White House conducts.

With political protectors surrounding him, the President was, in principle, shielded from prospective infiltrators who might not be people the Leader of the Free World could trust and depend on. However, Reagan was compact in his decision making and restrained in the number of people he let into his thought process, and he had less of a need to listen to and trust advisors. His instincts were most important to him, and together with his closest advisors—who managed day-to-day events, his schedule, and policy decisions—he was removed from personnel skirmishes that could distract him. As Chief of Staff, Jim Baker was superb at protecting Reagan from unwarranted challenges from Administration players who might make a misstep that would reflect adversely on his boss.

There were officials who did veer off the Reagan reservation, such as David Stockman, the disenchanted budget director; Col. Oliver North, the overly-ambitious engineer of the Iran-Contra deal; and Donald Regan, who as Reagan's Chief of Staff earned the fatal ire of the First Lady. But Reagan's eight years were largely free of the amount of internal political intrigue experienced by the Nixon or Clinton White Houses. This is not to say there was no competition at the staff level. Competition was in play, for example, in the movement of one of Reagan's closest friends, Bill Clark, to his position as Secretary of the Interior from his perch as National Security Advisor—where he had an office one floor below his friend the President—as well as in the scuttling of Secretary of State Al Haig completely from the Cabinet; he was replaced by George Shultz early in the first year.

CHAPTER TEN

Risk Taker

In May 1985 Reagan accepted the invitation of German Chancellor Helmut Kohl to attend a memorial ceremony at Kolmeshöhe Cemetery in Bitburg, West Germany, near the then capital of Bonn, where Reagan was to attend a G-5 Summit of world leaders. After Reagan's closest aide, Mike Deaver, had completed his preadvance trip to Germany and approved this event for the President's schedule, it was discovered that not only were there no American soldiers buried there, as Mike had been told there were, but there were SS soldiers interred in the cemetery. The SS had been declared not only a criminal organization but was named as directly responsible for the deaths of millions of Jews. Despite widespread controversy about the visit, including protests from military personnel, the notable Elie Wiesel, and others, Reagan, true to his word, refused to turn his back on Kohl and the decision he had made to accept the invitation. It was a question of honor and loyalty to him. He maintained the position that Kohl had taken considerable heat over the deployment of Western missile sites in Germany and he had stood by Reagan. Reagan was also well aware of the controversy and its possible short-term cost to his presidency as well as the amount of lobbying under way by many people, including his wife, to convince him to change his mind and cancel the Bitburg stop. It was a tough decision, and Reagan alone had to make it.

Once on the trip, Reagan spent a total of eight minutes in a brief ceremony at the cemetery and then he visited a concentration camp to honor Holocaust victims—a stop that had been added to the trip after the Bitburg controversy erupted. Reagan had the strength of character and the obstinacy to stick with a commitment he had made to Kohl, and he stood apart from those enmeshed in the day-to-day political controversy about this trip. Although protestors tried to make a larger issue of Reagan's going to Bitburg at the expense of possibly angering his Jewish constituents back home, it was well known that Reagan was a strong supporter of Israel and the American Jewish community. Turning the controversy into an advantage gave Reagan an opportunity to say some things that would not necessarily have ever been broadcast worldwide from a location like this. Had the media not promoted the dispute and escalated it to a controversial topic, Reagan would not have had such an unusual platform from which to sermonize with so many journalists reporting on it.

Here is a portion of what he said at Bitburg on a cold and gray day that everyone, at the staff level at least, really wanted over as quickly as possible:

"There are over 2,000 buried in Bitburg cemetery. Among them are 48 members of the SS—the crimes of the SS must rank among the most heinous in human history—but others buried there were simply soldiers in the German Army. How many were fanatical followers of a dictator and willfully carried out his cruel orders? And how many were conscripts, forced into service during the death throes of the Nazi war

machine? We do not know. Many, however, we know from the dates on their tombstones, were only teenagers at the time. There is one boy buried there a week before his 16th birthday.

"There were thousands of such soldiers to whom Nazism meant no more than a brutal end to a short life. We do not believe in collective guilt. Only God can look into the human heart, and all these men have now met their supreme judge, and they have been judged by Him as we shall all be judged.

"Our duty today is to mourn the human wreckage of totalitarianism, and today in Bitburg cemetery we commemorated the potential good in humanity that was consumed back then, 40 years ago."

Reagan's decision to make this trip to Bitburg was his own. He shouldered the political risk, although he could not have known about the list of soldiers interred there when the invitation was accepted. In this brief speech he took additional risks and plainly accepted responsibility for going there. Among the risks in this speech was the surprisingly bold statement *"We do not believe in collective guilt."* This was Reagan bringing up a subject debated for decades and still debated in Germany today. And yet Reagan takes the risk by making the startling pronouncement that *"only God can look into the human heart."* Who can say that but a clergyman? Here is a President representing a country that, with its allies, defeated a rampaging and murderous German regime, one that had set the world on end and launched a war during which there were sixty million deaths. Yet he stood and looked at the tombs of its fallen victims and criminals and announced that only God could perceive what is in a man's heart.

At another point, much earlier—and while in campaign mode—Reagan took a smaller but telling risk in a way that also paid off for him. During the 1980 presidential campaign, the *Nashua (NH) Telegraph* had offered to organize and broadcast a one-on-one debate between Reagan and George H. W. Bush. Reagan's campaign organization stepped up to pay for the event. When the editor of the paper, John Breen, attempted to turn off the amplification so that Reagan's criticism of the debate format (which Reagan felt should include *all* the candidates) could not be heard, Reagan spontaneously and angrily called Breen out by yelling "I am paying for this mic"—a line Reagan cleverly parroted from the 1948 movie *State of the Union*. People generally like a strong voice leading them. In this case, the way Reagan handled the situation was memorable and widely reported, and it helped Reagan secure the New Hampshire primary vote. *Time* magazine analyzed it this way: "The Reagan landslide surprised many of the hundreds of reporters who flooded the state the final week of the campaign. Although much attention has been accorded the 'Saturday Night Massacre' in Nashua, in which Bush had sided with the *Nashua Telegraph* in refusing to permit Anderson, Baker, Crane, and Dole to join a prearranged debate with Reagan, the Reagan resurgence was a broader phenomenon. The Nashua affair was only the most publicized portion of it." As Reagan campaign manager John Sears noted after the incident, "The debate was just a tremendous happening."

As the well-known Reagan biographer Craig Shirley, author of the book *Rendezvous with Destiny*, recalled, "Though the event had not been televised live, the networks and local news ran footage, repeatedly, of a frozen Bush and the booming Reagan. Most of New Hampshire's voters probably saw the film at least once. Three days later, Ronald Reagan won the New Hampshire primary in a completely unexpected blowout... He had staved off what had seemed his sure political sudden death."

In this relatively small but historic illustration, Reagan was exhibiting the type of moral strength he converted into power. His ire worked, because it was backed by the facts in this situation and it brought undecided supporters to his side. He had been dishonestly manipulated. Reagan was in the right, and people perceived this. Had he become angry over an issue where he was not perceived as correct, it could have backfired and detracted from this power. Strength and power are components of leadership; however, they can also be betrayers of leadership when not allied to fundamental values of honesty, integrity, and transparency. Coming out strong for ideals and explaining them convincingly enhances the individual. Coming out strong for purely personal aggrandizement or personal control may ultimately be acknowledged as weakness, foolishness, and failure—and while it may be temporarily dazzling and mesmerizing, it may be destructive and delusional.

Reagan's signature accomplishment involved his accepting the most risk and yielded the greatest reward—and this was his effort to help accelerate the disintegration of what had been America's most dominant enemy during the long Cold War: the Soviet Union. He sought not only to help free millions suffering under its totalitarian regime but to significantly lessen the fear that a generation of Americans themselves lived under. After all, they had constructed home bomb shelters and held civil defense drills in schools to protect themselves against genuinely felt threats made by aggressive Soviet scare tactics in the 1950s. This triumph did not come about through passive indifference or confusion over ideals and policy on his part. It came about through his assertive leadership and a persuasive influence on his team to come along with him for the ride.

I remember as an elementary school student participating in

civil defense drills and always noticing the yellow-and-black sign that led us to a safe place to hide in case of an attack by the Soviets. I also remember my parents discussing whether or not to build a bomb shelter in our yard and knowing families in the community who had. Reagan also knew that, although his strategy required an intermediate and expensive buildup of defense spending, if he was successful at actually lowering the probability of war, that could translate into an ultimate reduction of demands on the federal treasury.

Here Reagan talked in an unvarnished way about the Soviet menace in his March 1983 "Evil Empire" speech:

"During my first press conference as President in answer to a direct question, I pointed out that, as good Marxist-Leninists, the Soviet leaders have openly and publicly declared that the only morality they recognize is that which will further their cause, which is world revolution. I think I should point out I was only quoting Lenin, their guiding spirit, who said in 1920 that they repudiate all morality that proceeds from supernatural ideas—that's their name for religion—or ideas that are outside class conceptions. Morality is entirely subordinate to the interests of class war. And everything is moral that is necessary for the annihilation of the old, exploiting social order and for uniting the proletariat.

"Well, I think the refusal of many influential people to accept this elementary fact of Soviet doctrine illustrated an historical reluctance to see totalitarian powers for what they are. We saw the phenomenon in the 1930s. We see it too often today."

Reagan took the Soviet threat seriously. In these remarks he intermingles his understanding of religion, morality, freedom, evil, and destiny (his beliefs) and lays them against the bare and plain facts of Marxism-Leninism (the problem) for a specific educational and political purpose (policy or political objectives) while seeking a solution (action, results). I think Reagan saw himself as a torchbearer alerting people to what evil could happen if good people did nothing. Were other people also saying these things at the time and taking a similar risk in doing so? Yes, but to Reagan these violations against humanity were actionable, and he was ready to do something about it. He had the platform and the power of effective communication as well as his position as a head of state to help him deliver his message and carry out his goals.

Reagan saw himself as a missionary, which is reflected in the way he preached about and led on certain issues. He expected results from his messages. In this case, Reagan called out what the Soviets were trying to do and had, in effect, already accomplished to some extent. This was truth telling at its most dramatic. This doesn't mean that everyone believed him or even moved to his side of the aisle. People would obviously see and hear what Reagan believed, said, and warned about through their own subjective experiences and political predispositions.

His second major public policy objective and call to action was to help bolster what he considered to be the most effective way to lift people out of poverty—by accelerating economic opportunity and jobs in the private sector while reducing taxes. Reagan believed that growing government entitlements only created a new form of dependence, binding people to government for their personal and economic security. Reagan would never give up his belief that individual self-esteem comes through a productive role in society and by accepting individual responsibility to the extent humanly or physically possible. Reagan stuck with these basic principles throughout his eight years and was remembered for them. Here is how he put it in his First Inaugural Address in 1981:

> *"We are a nation that has a government—not the other way around.*

And this makes us special among the nations of the Earth. Our government has no power except that granted it by the people. It is time to check and reverse the growth of government, which shows signs of having grown beyond the consent of the governed.

"It is my intention to curb the size and influence of the Federal establishment and to demand recognition of the distinction between the powers granted to the Federal Government and those reserved to the States or to the people. All of us need to be reminded that the Federal Government did not create the States; the States created the Federal Government.

"Now, so there will be no misunderstanding, it's not my intention to do away with government. It is rather to make it work—work with us, not over us; to stand by our side, not ride on our back. Government can and must provide opportunity, not smother it; foster productivity, not stifle it."

He saw the overreach of government, through excessive regulation and its never-ending upward spiral of expansion, as an inhibitor to private sector job creation. He excoriated growing government entitlements for taking too much money out of the pockets of hard-working Americans. He was the exceptional Republican who could state these objectives in a way that average Americans could understand. He believed that for democracy to thrive, each individual had to have the freedom and the ability to achieve to their highest ability. The way Reagan demonstrated these beliefs was through his foreign and domestic policies and his legislative initiatives to cut taxes, freeze and lower Federal spending, reduce burdensome regulation, transfer some social programs to the States, reform welfare, simplify the tax code, strengthen the military, and fund the Strategic Defense Initiative. These were all risks with differing levels of political cost associated with them.

Let's look at the way Reagan expressed a 1982 call to action in his own words—his defense of a strong military and the critical importance of an America that supports fledgling democracies throughout the world:

"The march of freedom and democracy ... will leave Marxism-Leninism on the ash heap of history as it has left other tyrannies which stifle the freedom and muzzle the self-expression of the people. And that's why we must continue our efforts to strengthen NATO even as we move forward with our Zero-Option initiative in the negotiations on intermediate-range forces and our proposal for a one-third reduction in strategic ballistic missile warheads.

"Our military strength is a prerequisite to peace, but let it be clear we maintain this strength in the hope it will never be used, for the ultimate determinant in the struggle that's now going on in the world will not be bombs and rockets, but a test of wills and ideas, a trial of spiritual resolve, the values we hold, the beliefs we cherish, the ideals to which we are dedicated."

This is pure Reagan, linking his beliefs to the big issues of his time and expecting something to happen as a result. He sees warfare and talks about it as a conflict of belief systems and ideals and not just a clash of nuclear warheads. This is taking the problem of war to a more fundamental level than a consideration of material weaponry. In his speeches, like this one, focused on a strong defense, he is educating and advocating as much as anything else, while preparing for possible military action.

He said this about his domestic agenda in 1985 at the Great Valley Corporate Center in Malvern, Pennsylvania:

"Our tax cuts in 1981 lifted our economy out of—you've heard the word back then—'malaise' and into an almost 2½ years of growth. If those tax cuts could take a sick economy suffering from runaway inflation, skyrocketing interest rates, declining investments, sinking morale,

and slumping initiative and turn it into the strongest, most dynamic, and innovative economy in the world, think what America's tax plan can do today. We can build success on top of success. We can ignite the second stage of our booster rockets and blast this economy to new heights of achievement. We can do it and we will do it."

In this speech Reagan called for action but also ended it in a way that illustrated one of his strongest beliefs—that anything is possible. His optimism put a capstone on a talk that encouraged the listener to think that they *could* do or achieve anything. Reagan felt that if the leader held that the future would be bright—and he convinced his audience this was true—he was coalescing and harnessing a more powerful citizenry to build that future.

Courage and Risk Are Partners

There are different types of courage, moral and physical being the most widely recognized. John F. Kennedy, accepted into the military in World War II through his father's connections at the Defense Department, despite his being disqualified because of chronically poor health, performed heroic acts of physical courage that were later politically useful. When the wooden-hulled PT boat he was commanding was cut in half by a Japanese destroyer and sank, he swam many long hours in shark-infested Pacific Ocean waters to save the lives of some of his crewmembers and reach land. His actions earned him special recognition from the military, gave his family long-sought-for notice and respect, and provided him genuine political capital as well—especially when the story of his heroism became a book and then a movie seen by millions.

Churchill wrote that "courage is rightly esteemed the first of human qualities . . . because it is the quality which guarantees all others." I have also heard it said, "Leadership is the delivery of moral courage." During Reagan's years running the Screen Actors Guild, he received threats of physical violence warning him that communists would put an end to his film career by throwing acid on his face. That didn't stop him from his work for the union, but it did prompt him to take measures to protect himself. Threats like that, although less vivid, reoccurred throughout his career, and he did not acquiesce from the public stands he took at that time.

Reagan had to summon his own courage on numerous occasions himself. He was, for example, hospitalized and suffering from a rare form of pneumonia that left him near death on the day that his wife, Jane Wyman, delivered a baby girl named Christine. The baby died one day after her birth. Soon after that he was hit with a devastating divorce from Wyman, ending what was promoted as a fairy-tale marriage. His film career, during which he had been a top box-office draw, came to an end following WWII and he took a humiliating job in Las Vegas as a floor show host to earn a living. He lost primary elections in 1968 and 1976. I think these challenges to his pride kept Reagan humble and reinforced his well-placed trust in a Higher Power. He was not exempt from trouble, but he picked himself up and worked toward a better future for himself and his family.

A notable by-product of this courage is that he never liked to talk about his adversity, and he didn't need to in order to gain public support. He didn't aim to win sympathy; he aimed to earn confidence. Some politicians think that sharing every aspect of personal disability or misfortune is a way to garner popular support. Most audiences see through this, and if they don't, their support is sometimes a short-lived curiosity. Because Reagan had been through these troubles and survived, he knew that most other people had troubles as well, and he did not want to appear superior to them just because he had conquered his challenges and came out as a survivor.

In August 1981 public employees who were members of the Professional Air Traffic Controllers Organization walked off the job. Several months of contract negotiations and mediation had failed. Reagan took a calculated risk but decided to fire all of them. It was a decisive and historic move, and it helped set a cap on inflationary pressures from public labor union disputes in the following seven years of his presidency. He drew a line repudiating the right of public employees—especially those critical to transportation and other vital services—to strike. Reagan took strikers right to the edge, hoping for a negotiated settlement, but in the end he stuck with his commitment to fire them if they did not return to work. He humanely gave the controllers who went out on strike time to change their minds without any mark against their careers. In the end, they did not come back and lost their jobs. In the aftermath it took several years to fill these positions with newly trained, similarly qualified controllers. Another outcome was that public employee unions knew Reagan meant business and would not tolerate anyone walking off the job. What he earned went far beyond a victory with this particular union, however. This decision accrued to his public standing as a leader of strength, conviction, and courage. It was a risk well worth taking because of its perception as a win for the consumer.

In another risk-taking move, Reagan walked away from Gorbachev at the Reykjavik, Iceland, summit rather than acceding to Soviet demands that he end his research on the Strategic Defense Initiative. Abruptly exiting that summit meeting was a high-risk strategy. It included a willingness to accept what was described by the media as a defeat at the time. But Reagan knew differently, even as he was walking out. He knew it was another opportunity to show the Soviets that he would not give in to their demands when they were counter to the long-term American public interest and desire for peace. His walking out of that meeting was absolutely critical to what he was able to achieve later on. Nevertheless at the time, it subjected him to severe criticism, disappointment, and doubt about his leadership. As it turned out, it strengthened his hand with the Soviets and also confirmed that he was not always controlled by his advisors. His decision to walk out on Gorbachev was all his own. He alone stood for what he thought was strategically and morally right. His goals were the desires of the American and Russian people for lasting peace and security. He was walking out for them.

A risky venture that did not turn out well for Reagan was the 1985 Iranian arms-for-hostages deal. Reagan admitted to the commission investigating this episode and to the American people in televised Oval Office speeches that he did authorize an enterprise to help free hostages. On the use of funds from these arms sales to Israel and ultimately to Iran he stated he was unaware, and he had not authorized this abuse of the Boland Amendment, which effectively blocked military or financial support to freedom fighters in Nicaragua. As a result of the inquiry, fourteen Reagan administration officials were indicted and several resigned, including Bud McFarlane, his National Security Advisor. The Tower Commission concluded that Reagan had not exercised enough management control over the National Security Council in allowing one of its senior officers, Col. Oliver North, to make decisions regarding the Contras virtually on his own.

In 1982 the United States was hit with a severe recession. There were protests against Reagan's economic and social policies—many organized directly across the street from the White House in Lafayette Park and within earshot of the First Family. My office was on the south side of the White House, where it was relatively quiet, but when I was up in the family quarters, I could hear the protestors very well. On the road, while traveling, we were often confronted with picketers during this period. In these protests Reagan, as many Presidents before him, could observe firsthand the political costs of the actions he was taking with a political and economic agenda that did not start paying off until 1983.

Homelessness was another highly visible issue in the early 1980s caused in part by a decade-long government deinstitutionalization policy discharging chronically, mentally ill patients from large hospitals and care facilities. The goal was to mainstream them and integrate them into local communities. It was also a problem that was exacerbated by the Reagan recession. States, in cost-saving measures and because of the direction of social welfare trends, shut down many of their expensive institutional programs in favor of initiatives to treat those with mental disabilities in neighborhoods closer to their families and in smaller centers. This put more people on the streets.

Reagan was blamed for causing this problem and also preventing funding for solutions to long-term homelessness. In point of fact, however, this trend had started long before he arrived in Washington—during the Gerald Ford

Administration—and was largely a State's issue and not a Federal one. Nevertheless America is a place where all the nation's ills and crises accrue to the person in charge at the time they happen.

Homelessness, though a highly visible and tragic problem, has never been easy to solve, as so many communities have discovered. Reagan's solutions for it were grounded in his belief that local and state governments, churches, and nonprofits should address this chronic problem rather than the Federal government. Reagan was willing to shoulder the responsibility for tackling the economy and how unemployment affected homelessness. His partners would have to be states and municipalities.

CHAPTER ELEVEN

American Exceptionalism and the Role of Government

In Reagan's earliest days as a public speaker he was invited to deliver a commencement speech at a little known women's school then called William Woods College located in Fulton, Missouri. It was the same college where, at an earlier time in 1946, Winston Churchill delivered his lengthy and now iconic "Iron Curtain" speech. This address gave a name—the Cold War—to the rising noncombat aggression then stirring. This was how Churchill stated it:

"The United States stands at this time at the pinnacle of world power. It is a solemn moment for the American democracy. For with this primacy in power is also joined an awe-inspiring accountability to the future. As you look around you, you must feel not only the sense of duty done, but also you must feel anxiety lest you fall below the level of achievement. Opportunity is here now, clear and shining, for both our countries. To reject it or ignore it or fritter it away will bring upon us all the long reproaches of the after-time.

"It is necessary that constancy of mind, persistency of purpose, and the grand simplicity of decision shall rule and guide the conduct of the English-speaking peoples in peace as they did in war. We must, and I believe we shall, prove ourselves equal to this severe requirement."

Six years after Churchill addressed the student body there, Reagan began his own speech with a call on America never to abandon its global leadership responsibility amid rising tensions with the Soviets. As Reagan spoke to the graduates, he drew on his years in Hollywood in the heat of debates over communism. Even then Reagan was on fire about his conviction that the communism referred to by Churchill was an active and evil force. That may be what motivated him to show these graduates an early version of Reagan the evangelist. In his speech, lost and disregarded for decades, Reagan started by calling America, significantly, *"less of a place than an idea,"* and continued by answering what this idea might be:

"It is nothing but the inherent love of freedom in each one of us . . . [which is] the basis of this country . . . the idea of the dignity of man, the idea that deep within the heart of each one of us is something so godlike and precious that no individual or group has a right to impose his or its will upon the people, . . . so well as they can decide for themselves."

Forty years later, Reagan returned to this theme of a nation of ideas and ideals when, as ex-President at age eighty-one, he addressed the 1992 Republican Convention:

"There was a time when empires were defined by land mass, subjugated peoples, and military might. But the United States is unique, because we are an empire of ideals. For two hundred years we have been set apart by our faith in the ideals of democracy, of free men and free markets, and of the extraordinary possibilities that lie within seemingly ordinary men and women."

For Reagan, American goodness and exceptionalism were not the whole story. It was America's historic and special purpose, its Constitution, its place in the forward march of civilization and human progress that mattered most to him. He viewed history in a dynamic way and saw every aspect of it as deliberate and fundamental to its future. Reagan was always hopeful, so it would be natural for him to think that America's best days were always ahead and something to expect and strive for. I think he viewed history like a conveyor belt moving the world toward better days and social and economic improvement, and to the degree that anyone got on this conveyor belt and rode that engine, they benefited from its forward progress into the future. And why not adopt this view? It may seem simplistic to some but for those whose lives had been saved and improved by the American way of life, and there have been many millions who fall in this category, every word of Reagan's belief had meaning, but more importantly it had its proof. For those who had not yet benefited from it, it was just as important to keep the prospect of economic improvement in front of them. That is one reason Reagan had a reach and appeal across the political and economic spectrum, as seen in the number of Democrats who voted for him. Political parties may be adrift today because they have done a poor job of adopting this big-tent approach. Optimism can result in empowerment. Reagan himself was an example of that.

Reagan was a product of America, and America was in his blood. He could have had a permanent tattoo on his forehead saying, "Made in America." He was raised in a series of small towns, in a semirural civic culture with Midwestern values of honesty, neighborliness, and hard work at the core. In the Reagan family's circle of friends, everyone was at the same economic level: poor and struggling. Outside of the moral support of his family, church, and community, he had nothing given to him. He had to earn every opportunity. He was also brought up in and influenced by a tradition of faith in a church that was founded in America. He lifted himself up professionally and economically from the poverty of his parents, and he had to create a new identity for himself as he went along.

While he carried the values and experiences of his boyhood with him throughout his life, at each stage of his career he had to assume a slightly modified persona to fit the requirements of the jobs he performed. He had natural leadership and communication abilities and was the second in his family, along with his older brother, Neil, to receive a college education. The first home his parents actually ever owned was in retirement—the one he bought for them in California after he became a film actor. Reagan lived the American dream. He was blessed by the opportunity his country afforded him, and he knew and acknowledged it. He felt he owed a debt to his country, and he wanted to pay it back by serving. This is how most members of the Greatest Generation felt about America.

Reagan knew the rules and he respected them, learned how to play by them, and how to use them for advancement. He never expected that just because he was raised with meager financial means, he would have to remain at that level. His mother made sure that her son Dutch, as he was nicknamed, knew that there was plenty of opportunity waiting for him if he would live a good life and aspire to greater things. I don't think it ever occurred to him that anyone else who wanted it and was able could not achieve as he did. He saw opportunity as an equal benefit for everyone. This led him to write, years later:

"The American dream is not that every man must be level with every other man. The American dream is that every man must be free to become whatever God intends he should become."

Americans are generally aware of the significant advantages of their country and are mindful of its shortcomings—while expectant that they can be remedied. But Reagan looked out at America and Americans, and where some leaders might see a nation's failings and are apologetic because of them, he saw a great nation founded on remarkable principles as well as people who were overwhelmingly kind, inventive, neighborly, and inherently good—and needing no apology. He talked about this in his speeches even before he assumed the presidency. To him the future held promise for its citizens and their families, and he set about telling Americans how good they were and how great their country was whenever he could. He saw his job, in part, to build up a nation's confidence in itself, in its ability to achieve and to make good on providing opportunity for everyone. What he believed in was American Exceptionalism.

Reagan said in 1985 at a ceremony celebrating Hispanic Heritage Week:

"At the root of everything that we're trying to accomplish is the belief that America has a mission. We are a nation of freedom, living under God, believing all citizens must have the opportunity to grow, create wealth, and build a better life for those who follow. If we live up to those moral values, we can keep the American dream alive for our children and grandchildren, and America will remain mankind's best hope."

Reagan spoke of America as the *"last best hope of man on earth,"* that *"our country's best days are ahead,"* and that America has a *"special purpose"* in world history. For him these were not just comforting and quaint aphorisms of a bygone era. They illustrated the pride and esteem in which this President held his country. This belief wasn't just a turn of phrase for Reagan. It formed the basis for every policy and every action he took while in office. He was an evangelist for America, not for imperialist reasons but for idealistic ones. He fought for the spread and expansion of democratic freedoms throughout the world, but not for political annexation or territorial expansion. He genuinely felt that the hallmarks of American-style democracy would accord every human being on the face of the earth the personal freedoms and the liberty they deserved. He wanted the whole world to share in it. He was an unrepentant, unapologetic idealist and optimist. He loved his country.

Reagan did not believe in the superiority of the American people, its culture, its business, industry, or art relative to other cultures. He believed in the superiority of the principles on which American democracy was founded, and in the structure of its representative form of government with its transparency and checks and balances, and he wanted these to be accessible to any nation that sought them.

This is a critical distinction lost on some who debate the Exceptionalism issue. Some have maintained that Exceptionalism means that Americans feel they are superior to people in other cultures around the globe in a chauvinistic or nationalistic way. This did not figure into Reagan's reasoning at all. He was a champion for worldwide democracy movements, but only because of what he believed they could achieve for everyone in the world. One specific example of this was his Caribbean Basin Initiative, which was designed to promote economic opportunity and to bolster fledgling democracies. This would both benefit the people of this region and also protect U.S. security interests in what was at that time a politically volatile part of the world, close to American shores and its economic interests.

National polling has consistently revealed that at times as many as 80 percent of all U.S. citizens believe in American Exceptionalism. When asked to define it, however, there were many different interpretations of it—ranging from superiority at sports and science to the values of freedom and liberty protected by the U.S. Constitution. Even though American Exceptionalism can be misinterpreted or distorted for political purposes, this belief brought President Kennedy to make the commitment to land a man on the moon and allowed an entire generation to dream of reaching that far-off destination. As Russel B. Nye noted in his book *This Almost Chosen People*, "The search by Americans for a precise definition of their national purpose, and their absolute conviction that they have such a purpose, provides one of the most powerful threads in the development of an American ideology." Americans do not have to go farther than our national Constitution to find that purpose—to see a country founded on nothing but ideals, the breadth of which had not been seen before.

Reagan felt that if the guiding light of American Exceptionalism were to dim, weaken, or go out entirely, the whole world would suffer from that darkness. He felt that America had no choice but to spread its light. To him it was a key ingredient in its founding principles and an obligation from which it gained its justification and strength as a nation. In other words, to him freedom for Americans without the prospect of freedom for every human being might constitute a threat to the security of the freedoms Americans themselves enjoy. This was a key point for Reagan. Isolationism was not an option for him. The global interventionism of American ideals was his primary goal, but he imagined the results in practical terms. Reagan kept up an unapologetic drumbeat of what America stood for in all his dealings with other nations, touting the ability of our democratic form of government to provide opportunity for anyone to lift themselves from poverty into economic stability.

For Reagan the role of the United States in the world originated from the teaching of man being his brother's keeper, the rule of law, and the responsibility to help advance the freedom that he felt was the innate right of every man, woman, and child. This policy also had its ramifications for the safety and security of Americans, because the more democracy there is in the world, the safer the United States may be from potential aggression, harm, and terror. The less freedom and democracy, the greater the threat to American security and its way of life, and the higher the cost—in dollars and human life— of defending it. Promoting and supporting democracy and freedom abroad are an effective defensive strategy and a good investment policy in our future.

I do not believe that Reagan saw America as the world's exclusive unilateral peacekeeper, even though he was skeptical of multilateral initiatives whereby the United States could possibly lose control of the governing principles. I think Reagan saw the United States as a peace igniter and in a standard-bearer role. Reagan held more bilateral meetings and worked harder at developing relations with the heads of other countries than most nonwartime Presidents. A record number of heads of state came to the White House during his eight years. At any given time we had long lists of requests through the State Department and the National Security Council of countries who wanted their heads of state to be welcomed by Reagan at the White House. It was a challenge to fit them all in the schedule, and some had to be accorded lesser-level "working" visits rather than official state visits with all the honors and ceremony they were accorded. Reagan's personal diplomacy skills were expert and critical to his achieving ambitious foreign policy goals. He was adept at establishing productive friendships with other heads of state. Communication with these leaders was a high priority for him, and he knew developing strong ties between leaders could improve the world condition and lessen the threat of strife.

The Reagans hosted at least one foreign head of state at the White House per month. My office managed many elements of these visits and it was my responsibility to direct aspects of the events that occurred during these visits. During these ceremonies, I worked closely with the President. We would discuss the details prior, during, and after the state visits. I saw his pride at introducing his guests to American hospitality and White House tradition. I also saw his genuine interest in his guests and their backgrounds, human interests, points of view, and of course bilateral and multilateral diplomatic agendas. I could also see his guests warming to Reagan and appreciating his invitations.

In 1974 Reagan said: *"We cannot escape our destiny, nor should we try to do so. The leadership of the free world was thrust upon us two centuries ago in that little hall of Philadelphia. In the days following World War II, when the economic strength and power of America was all that stood between the world and the return to the dark ages, Pope Pius XII said, 'The American people have a great genius for splendid and unselfish actions. Into the hand of America God has placed the destinies of an afflicted mankind.' "*

In some ways Reagan was really a gentleman of an earlier era, and he identified with earlier American Presidents much more than his more immediate predecessors. After all, many of these earlier leaders were, to him, legendary thinkers and doers working in the national interest. They glimpsed the possibilities the new country offered and strove to achieve them. Some of his heroes served when America was nothing but an undeveloped land of opportunity facing a promising but uncertain future.

Because Reagan valued the lives and record of the Founders and earlier American leaders, it was natural for him to adopt as his own the image of America put forth by one of its Pilgrim leaders. The *"shining city on a hill"* metaphor, pronounced on the deck of the tiny ship *Arabella* in Plymouth Harbor by a future Governor of Massachusetts, John Winthrop, was a natural and convenient one for Reagan to take as his own. It was also purposeful on Reagan's part. He was employing a parable and someone else's words to convey a message in ways that were both symbolic and visually engaging. By depicting what he saw as America's destiny, he was also drawing a distinction between the United States and governments that did not earn his respect. He felt that the more people knew about and understood the American model of democracy, the easier it would be for them to abandon those forms of government not based on the ideals of individual freedom and liberty.

The "shining city" quote is a reference, not only to John Winthrop, but to the book of Matthew, chapter 5, verses 14–16. These verses refer not only to the light of the metaphoric city but also to the responsibility of the follower to carry and reflect this light for the benefit of the world. For Reagan, this linking of light and of American destiny was not his own brand of ardent nationalism. For him this gift of freedom and light was never bestowed by the state but was inherent in its founding principles and sustained by the spirit of its people.

In the same 1992 speech where Reagan defined Exceptionalism, he told the audience a story about optimism. After referring to America as a country that is *"forever young,"* he said, *"A fellow named James Allen once wrote in his diary, 'Many thinking people believe America has seen its best days.' "* The trouble with that pessimistic sentiment, according to Reagan, was that Allen had written that in his diary on July 26, 1775! Perhaps for James Allen, the American Revolution had gotten off to a good start at Lexington and Concord, but by July the patriots were outgunned on land and at sea. They were fighting the mightiest empire on earth, and they were doing that with a ragtag bunch of militia men and without a real navy. It was no wonder Allen was pessimistic. But look at what had happened since then! Reagan went on in this speech to catalog a history of accomplishments, struggles, and triumphs that would convince any pessimist to reverse course and become an optimist.

This 1992 speech was called "America's Best Days Are Yet to Come," and while he was winding down his own life personally, he wanted to communicate the optimism he would forever associate with his country and to help imbue it with this eternal conviction. He implored,

"America's best days are yet to come. Our proudest moments are yet to be. Our most glorious achievements are just ahead." According to the way Reagan saw it, he shared Ralph Waldo Emerson's view that America was *"the country of tomorrow."*

One of the central planks in the Reagan 1980 presidential campaign platform was that government serves the people and not the other way around. To this end Reagan said:

"Let us all remember, ideas do matter. We didn't come to Washington to be caretakers of power. We weren't elected to become managers of the decline or just to see if we couldn't run the same old shop and maybe do it a little more efficiently. We were sent here to move America forward again by putting people back in charge of their own country, to promote growth . . . to give individuals the opportunities to reach for their dreams, to strengthen institutions of family, school, church, and

community, to make the United States a stronger leader for peace, free-dom, and progress abroad, and, through it all, to renew our faith in the God who has blessed our land."

For Reagan, the idea of government predominance, domination, or control, especially in a well-established, committed, and formal democracy, was anathema. In his mind it was the first step toward socialism and tyranny because it diminished the responsibility and thereby the capacity, fulfillment, and self-determination of the individual. He felt that freedom was built and maintained by individuals and that government gained its legitimacy from them collectively, not the other way around. He felt that only through preserving the rights and the power of the individual could freedom and progress be protected and passed down from generation to generation. His roots in the liberal Democratic Party and his clash with communism early in his career while serving as head of the Screen Actors Guild gave him a taste of something he saw as threatening to American-style democracy and government by the people.

What made Reagan's perspective unique was that to him the greatest evil of a government grown dominant over its people could be its potential to separate a man from his God and to deny access to Divine Providence by replacing it with dependence on and allegiance to an all-powerful state. This had occurred in his lifetime under communist regimes, where atheism was the state deity. His experiences in Hollywood after World War II directly affected his beliefs about welfare, government overregulation, and runaway spending, and they led to his policy initiatives designed to rein in the size and reach of government.

Reagan was not a policy wonk. He saw government or

public policy as a derivative of and subordinate to the will of the people in a democratic context. He effected policy but did not steep himself in it. He was more in the idea business and his idea was that the growth of government had to be eclipsed. He told the American people that at every opportunity he had. It was not an easy task, however, to rein in the sprawl and span of overreaching government, and his success at it as President was limited and his efforts for reform met with mixed results. What he can be credited with is bringing the idea to the forefront of the public debate and keeping up an unyielding drumbeat for these principles. By employing these principles he launched a Reagan doctrine that lives on but is not completely understood or adhered to by politicians today.

During his two terms, there were commissions and studies on reducing the size of government, initiatives to improve government efficiency, campaigns for the presidential line-item veto, and some of these met with modest success. There were government hiring freezes, agency size reductions, furloughs, RIFs (reductions in force), budgetary congressional showdowns where the government was actually shut down, and other specific tactics to conquer this problem. Some measure of success could be accorded to Reagan, but what is remembered was his hammering these positions into the political history of America and its collective consciousness. Looking back, it could always be said that Reagan stood for limited government and individual freedom.

In his farewell address from the Oval Office in January 1989, he was ready to claim a limited victory over government's unending expansion. In his parting remarks he said:

"Ours was the first revolution in the history of mankind that truly reversed the course of government, and with three little words . . . 'We

the People' tell the government what to do; it doesn't tell us . . . 'We the People' are the driver; the government is the car. And we decide where it should go, and by what route, and how fast."

In this last address, Reagan chose to talk about the relationship of a people to its government just as he had in his 1981 inaugural address. Before he closed his remarks he went back to the Constitution and repeated again and again the phrase that gave this belief its lifeblood: *"We the People. We the People."* He had started out in this first inaugural address laying down the gauntlet: Government must *"work with us, not over us; [it must] stand by our side, not ride on our back. Government . . . must provide opportunity, not smother it; foster productivity, not stifle it."*

CHAPTER TWELVE

Rebuilding American Strength

Reagan was shocked by what he found when he arrived in Washington as President. This was especially true of what he discovered about our nation's defense and military capacity, morale, and readiness. He understood the cost of military vulnerability, and he saw the future threat of terrorism years before 9/11. He said on December 27, 1983:

"The thrust of the history of this country is that we've recognized a clear distinction between being at peace with other states and being at war. We have never before faced a situation in which others routinely sponsor and facilitate acts of violence against us while hiding behind proxies and surrogates which . . . they claim they do not fully control . . .

"In the days ahead we need to systematically redevelop our approach to this problem, recognizing that the worst outcome of all is one in which terrorists succeed in transforming an open democracy into a closed fortress . . . We have to come to grips with the fact that today's terrorists are better armed and financed, they are more sophisticated, they are possessed by a fanatical intensity that individuals of a democratic society can only barely comprehend."

It is common knowledge that Reagan presided over the biggest peacetime military buildup in U.S. history. This included the development and deployment of new technology platforms and components, designing and manufacturing new precision weaponry, and, also important, military pay increases. In his first five years in office, Pentagon expenditures for defense spending doubled from $143 billion to $287 billion. This buildup was a part of Reagan's plan to bring down the Soviet system and its policy of global expansionism by addressing the alarming problems in our own military—what he recounted as *"planes that couldn't fly for lack of spare parts; ships that couldn't leave port; and helicopters that couldn't stay aloft."* His overall military goal for the United States was to bankrupt the Soviets in an arms race designed to hold their attention and to underscore the seriousness with which Reagan took his leadership and his campaign to rid the world of communism.

Reagan did not undertake this massive buildup because he wanted to go to war. He did it precisely so that America would *not* go to war. Reagan was also able to persuade a doubting Congress to pay for the weapons systems that were later used in both Persian Gulf wars; they were not fought on his watch but were won by the weaponry developed during it. To mention but a few accomplishments of the Defense Department under Reagan: The Navy returned to its full force (525 ships) through an aggressive shipbuilding campaign and superb leadership of Secretary John Lehman; the Air Force developed the stealth technology that later forced Saddam Hussein out of Kuwait in 1992; the introduction of the Army's M-1 tanks that eventually went into Baghdad twelve years later to bring down Hussein's regime; and the unveiling of the Apache helicopter. Many nations were watching this buildup and assessing it in terms of their own military strength. Reagan said, poignantly,

"History teaches that war begins when governments believe the price of aggression is cheap."

When he arrived in Washington, Reagan was handed a Defense Department afflicted with racial, drug, and alcohol problems as well as difficulties recruiting enough qualified soldiers. The number of recruits coming into the military prior to Reagan's inauguration was the lowest in a decade. The military had also been hard hit by years of neglect from an unpopular Vietnam War. Morale was at a low point. Reagan's Army Chief of Staff said that "the military...needed to be told by the top person that they were honored and appreciated."

Reagan did that in spades. He loved men and women in uniform, had enormous respect for them, and assumed an attitude of humility and gratitude any time military personnel saluted him. When I traveled with him, often landing at U.S. military bases around the world, as well as every time Air Force One took off or landed at Andrews Air Force Base just outside Washington, DC, I could see that Reagan was eager to show those in the military how much he respected them and supported them, and how much the entire country appreciated their extreme sacrifices. This was a big part of Reagan's character—his appreciation for and devotion to the men and women who served in the military.

There is not a trip I take today where I meet men and women in uniform or distinguished retired military officers who do not share their profound respect and admiration for President Reagan. He was their man and he engendered their confidence—as a leader and their Commander in Chief. They felt he was one who would defend them, which he did constantly in the U.S. Congress, just as they would defend him. As a result there was a mutual respect that was productive. Caspar Weinberger, who served as Reagan's Defense Secretary, said that Reagan "restored the military and turned around the morale almost overnight . . . we had more volunteers than we could enlist."

This military buildup was a part of a move away from the containment strategy (of Soviet aggression) to what Weinberger called "a war that needs to be won . . . In order to do what we had to, to regain our strength." In a way it was almost as if Reagan was getting another chance to see the active duty that had eluded him fully in World War II—when he was grounded after enlisting because of poor eyesight. He put himself squarely with the military service men and women. The military returned Reagan's respect and investment in them, their families, and their fighting conditions and preparedness, with their deep respect for him. Reagan said of the military buildup, *"Of the four wars in my lifetime, none came about because the United States was too strong."* And during one of his radio addresses in 1987 he said *"Well, one of the worst mistakes anybody makes is to bet against Americans."*

The rebuilding of America's strength in the world was not exclusively the responsibility of the Department of Defense. The Department of State was also fully engaged in strengthening its diplomacy and attempting to turn from apologizing to plain speaking and truth telling. George Shultz, Reagan's longest serving Secretary of State and friend from his California days, was a full partner with the President in his campaign to bring about the downfall of Soviet communism. Shultz brought important and sometimes divergent views to the President about how his goals would best be accomplished.

Reagan was best able to articulate how this campaign would be won, and it was a complex plan based on simple facts and beliefs and he was the indisputable leader and chief strategist.

He kept his goal in sight and proceeded on a strenuous and undeviating timeline. He needed the expertise of every foot soldier, as he would call the Reaganites, but he knew instinctively what had to be done.

Even the domestic policy programs Reagan proposed and supported, starting with the Private Sector Initiatives program, figured in strengthening democracy's fabric to help accelerate an end to totalitarianism. It was as if he was working on a thousand-piece puzzle and Reagan alone had the vision of what the final picture would look like. Reagan recognized that he needed not only the Reaganites who had signed on to work for him but an army of Americans, newly awakened to what he saw as internal and external threats to democracy. He knew he needed to strengthen America's faith in itself as well as provide the physical weaponry to maintain its standing in the world. Reagan knew, as any leader must, that the primary buildup had to be one of confidence in the internal system, and when that was accomplished, it would provide the strongest immunity against unfriendly fire of any type. Reagan was himself cut from American cloth, and he knew America's greatness started and ended in homes, neighborhoods, and local communities. This morale boosting was as much of his defense strategy as the humming of munitions factories.

Another important Reagan trademark was his adoption of the old Russian proverb that translated into English as "Trust But Verify." Reagan learned this from his exceptional Russian cultural tutor, Suzanne Massie, and he put it to good use when addressing the Soviets—so much so that Gorbachev complained about Reagan's overuse of it. Nevertheless the Soviet leader got the point. This was a natural statement for Reagan to use. It represented his character perfectly. He was naturally trusting but adopted, by necessity, a sufficient degree of skepticism—especially when related to the Soviets, because he knew they rarely completely honored treaties and foreign policy agreements. It was an apt adage and more than superficial when used in negotiations with the Soviet Union, because it was a phrase taken from their own cultural lexicon. Now it is a phrase owned and utilized more broadly in theatres of war or in negotiations of any type. It also sets a standard against which to secure the truth and verify it by the follow-up. It is the heart (trust) and the head (verify) working together. Reagan valued that syncopation.

Reagan's motto, "Peace Through Strength," was as much a moral banner as a military one. He justified a military buildup on a moral basis. Its goal was to defeat an immoral enemy. Military strength, for him, was a symbol of American willingness to defend what he saw as the most humane system of rights and individual liberty the world had ever known. His battle was against any enemy that could weaken these American ideals.

CHAPTER THIRTEEN

Man of Modest Philanthropy
and Midwestern Warmth

Before he was elected President, and as if to show his faith in his country, his countrymen, and their humanity, Reagan said at a 1974 First Conservative Political Action Conference:

"Somehow America has bred a kindliness into our people unmatched anywhere . . . We are not a sick society. A sick society could not produce the men that set foot on the moon, or who are now circling the earth above us in the Skylab. A sick society bereft of morality and courage did not produce the men who went through those years of torture and captivity in Vietnam. Where did we find such men? They are typical of this land, as the Founding Fathers were typical. We found them in our streets, in the offices, the shops and the working places of our country and on the farms."

Throughout his eight years in the White House, Reagan was a practicing philanthropist, putting his beliefs into action in a quiet and modest manner. He would read about someone in need or suffering from adversity, or he would receive letters from people down on their luck, and he would send them a small donation. The President often composed a handwritten letter to accompany a personal check, placing them both in an envelope he addressed to be mailed personally by Kathy Osborne, his secretary.

In his book *In the President's Secret Service*, Ron Kessler quotes Frank J. Kelly, who drafted the President's messages: "Reagan was famous for firing up Air Force jets on behalf of children who needed transport for kidney operations... These are things you never knew about. He never bragged about it. I hand-carried checks for four thousand or five thousand dollars to people who had written him. He would say, *'Don't tell people. I was poor myself.'*" (Emphasis added.)

In 1983 the *New York Times* told the story of one man who had hung up on Reagan six times before being convinced it was in fact the President on the phone, who was calling to offer him help. "[It was] like talking to your favorite uncle," said Arlis Sheffield of Wakefield, Rhode Island. "He was very humble. You would never know he was president of the United States." Reagan was not in a financial position to make large donations, but he kept up a steady stream of smaller contributions where he could while promoting and acknowledging the power of giving to the American people.

Reagan found it difficult to make friends in early boyhood because of frequent household moves the family made from one rented apartment or house to another. This may also have affected his ability to forge deep, bonding friendships throughout his life. Yet despite this influence, he genuinely liked people. Reagan did not hold grudges against people. He just didn't have that in him. Revenge, for example, would not even have registered on Reagan's radar screen as something he would engage in, although politics is very often sadly practiced that way.

During the Christmas season at the White House, the Reagans hosted an endless stream of parties for various groups, and I was on duty for most of them. Then, and throughout the year, I observed the President close at hand while he would stand for hours in many receiving lines. I saw time after time how he would express delight over some small gesture expressed by a guest. Everyone was important to him. Even after exhausting duty in one of these lines, the President never expressed any fatigue or irritation—even with people who *were* irritating, like the unforgettable woman who showed up dressed from head to toe (including a turban) in a special polyester fabric woven with the name Reagan all over it in red, white, and blue, and a bolt of the stuff under her arm to try and sell to the President! She was sure he would want to buy it and she was equally as sure people would want to wear it!

After working these receiving lines Reagan would often tell me a story or joke that someone had told him in the line, and he typically had a twinkle in his eye when retelling it. He liked the American people, and he took delight in them—their humanity, their spirit, what they accomplished, and what they stood for. In a way he identified with them. He also admired them. Reagan was always telling his fellow citizens how good they were. As if to summarize his feelings about his fellow Americans on the eve of the 1984 election, Reagan said:

"The greatness of America doesn't begin in Washington; it begins with each of you—in the mighty spirit of free people under God, in the bedrock values you live by each day in your families, neighborhoods, and workplaces. Each of you is an individual worthy of respect, unique and important to the success of America. And only by trusting you, giving you opportunities to climb high and reach for the stars, can we preserve the golden dream of America as the champion of peace and freedom among the nations of the world."

I remember one evening where extraordinary humanity and American philanthropy blended in a potent force on the White House South Lawn, when the President hosted a heroic group of young Special Olympians with disabilities. To witness their overcoming of enormous physical handicaps to compete athletically was awe inspiring. They were assembled on the South Lawn of the White House to celebrate the twenty-fifth anniversary of this remarkable Kennedy family charity at a picnic in their honor. To the assembled group of athletes Reagan spoke these words:

"I understand that in Special Olympics, your torch is called the Flame of Hope. And that's exactly what your athletes represent today. By training and competing in these events, you're realizing your hopes for a fuller, more productive life. And you're kindling in the rest of us the hope that through individual effort we can make this a more caring world."

The President was equally generous in his praise and gratitude to the Kennedy family for forming and funding this life-changing example of American philanthropy at its best. Eunice Kennedy Shriver, the President of the family foundation, personally told me years later that that day profoundly affected her perception of Ronald Reagan, his character, kindness, humanity, and leadership qualities.

One of these unique and courageous athletes came up to and grabbed Reagan and held him in one long body hug. The President relished it. I was standing right next to him when this occurred, and I watched as the Secret Service allowed this to happen even though these body hugs were forceful, powerful grabs by muscled runners and wrestlers. Reagan was just as exuberant as the athletes and enjoyed this personal encounter with them. Seeing what the Kennedy family had done for these inspiring athletes and the connection Reagan made with them was genuinely moving and emotional for everyone there.

President Reagan's own American-style humanity and warmth were also on display when he traveled abroad, and they helped him boost a better understanding of and appreciation for American culture. His remarkable geniality was known by ordinary folks like the bartenders at the O'Farrell Pub in Ballyporeen, Ireland, where we dropped in one afternoon—every detail choreographed by the masterful Rick Ahearn of the White House advance office—during a two-day official visit to the country of Reagan's ancestry. Even with the elaborate staging and hundreds in the press pool observing, Reagan was able to sidle up to the middle of the well-worn, long wooden bar, while I watched him from the other end—well out of the photo. He was able to gain immediate rapport with the local pub-going community. Of course there was a lot of clamor and a fairly big crowd, but Reagan started asking everyone about life in the quaint village, where it is thought many O'Regans, the President's ancestors, are buried—all while he was served up a pint and downed it with his new friends. He honestly felt right at home and the pub goers could relate to Reagan because he was genuine and had a friendly disposition.

Reagan was generous and kind with people he met and showed them respect—and these locals were no exception. He was interested in their everyday life and history. I think he could have stayed on all afternoon with that crowd; however, as with all traveling heads of state, we had to move on—too quickly for Reagan's taste, I am sure. Today the authentic interior of that pub can be seen at the Reagan Library in Simi Valley, California, as a tribute to his historic visit to Ballyporeen, thanks to the generosity of Fred Ryan, the Library Chairman.

Reagan had no special vanity or pretention, and once people met him they felt that. He had no need to compete for attention. His age also might have contributed to a feeling of safety people felt with him—like your dad or grandfather was here and that everything would be all right after all. Then, too, he was comfortable in his own skin, and that drew people in. In 1983, Reagan dropped in at another pub—this one called the Eire in heavily Democratic Dorchester, Massachusetts— not exactly Reagan territory like Ballyporeen, Ireland, might have been. It was social hour, and Reagan dove right in with a few good stories and left with a posse of admirers—if not political converts. Among them, Mike Corbett, a construction worker, told reporters that while he didn't share Reagan's politics, he was nevertheless impressed with the fortieth President and summed up his thoughts by saying of Reagan that "he made an effort to reach out to people." Rich Bishkin, another Eire Pub regular, recalling Reagan's visit said, "He won over so many."

After Reagan's passing, journalist Brian Williams commented on a 2004 MSNBC television special that "there is general agreement about one thing: Ronald Wilson Reagan had a remarkable ability to connect with people—millions of Americans across the country." Listening to this pronouncement, I found myself remembering so many times I stood by and watched Reagan with people. Reagan's basic love for people, and his ability to see them as good and see the good in them, was the invisible radiation that made people think they were liked by Reagan—and they usually returned the favor, especially if they had an opportunity to meet him in person.

In June 2009, I delivered a speech in New York City. As I was leaving the stage, I was approached by a woman with tears streaming down her face. She caught up with me, and cautiously but emotionally, she began to tell me her dramatic story. She was a Russian immigrant who came to the United States under a 1983 accord brokered by Reagan for the release of a limited number of Jews from the Soviet Union. During my remarks I had spoken of the President and my honor at being able to work for him. "It was Reagan's words and the way he convincingly and emotionally spoke them that gave me hope—the only hope I had in the world—and ultimately led me to America," she said movingly. I learned from her later that she had earned a PhD in mathematics from Moscow University and had achieved almost overnight success as an investment banker upon reaching the United States.

She told me over and over again that she owed her life to Reagan and to his words, which she had heard broadcast through the U.S. Information Agency radio, at that time headed by the Reagans' longtime and close California supporter and personal friend, Charlie Wick. She recounted how she would listen to Reagan's messages of hope and freedom, and dream of a land where these ideals could become reality. Because of what Reagan said and how sincerely he said it, she actually pictured America as "some sort of heaven or paradise." Ultimately her dream came true, and she even credited Reagan with placing this dream in her heart, giving her the resolve to apply for immigration and paving the way for her to leave the Soviet Union.

Pastor John Boyles, who served on the ministerial staff of the National Presbyterian Church while Reagan was in office, shared with me his personal encounters with Reagan. He talked about his humanity and how the President valued it in American life. Boyles was asked by the President to establish and chair a Commission on Ethics in America, which he did enthusiastically over a number of years. Although mostly now forgotten, the panel included noted theologians, philanthropists, and writers.

Reagan also sent Reverend Boyles on a special private mission to Moscow in 1982 to check on the condition of the Siberian Seven, a family of Pentecostal Christians who had sought refuge at the U.S. Embassy. For five years this family lived in a room in the basement of Spaso House, the U.S. Embassy. Boyles told me he wore a wooden belt buckle that turned into a cross, which he gave them for encouragement. Along with this gift, he carried a personal message from the President.

Reagan's view of American humanity was not limited by race or religious distinction. When he was an undergraduate student at Eureka College traveling overnight with a football team, he saw his African-American teammates being shut out from the motel where the team was staying. He abruptly told the coach the team was leaving the hotel, and that his black colleagues would stay at his own house and have breakfast the next morning with his parents. Jack and Nelle Reagan had raised their two boys—who had both attended racially integrated public high schools—never to field a racial thought. They were forbidden from seeing the film *Birth of a Nation*, because it glorified the Ku Klux Klan. Reagan's dad, during his traveling salesman days, would also not stay at motels where Jews were not welcome. In Reagan's vision of America, everyone was entitled to equal rights, and, as with so much of his worldview, the origins of his beliefs in equality came from his understanding that all men are equal in the eyes of God. He insisted, in his 1992 convention speech:

"Whether we come from poverty or wealth; whether we are Afro-American or Irish-American; Christian or Jewish, from big cities or small towns, we are all equal in the eyes of God." He added importantly, *"But as Americans that is not enough. We must be equal in the eyes of each other. We can no longer judge each other on the basis of what we are, but must instead start finding out who we are. In America, our origins matter less than our destinations, and that is what democracy is all about."*

At the end of World War II Reagan spoke at the Santa Ana Municipal Bowl to protest hostility against returning Japanese-American veterans. He said:

"America stands unique in the world—a country not founded on race, but on a way and an ideal. Not in spite of, but because of our polyglot background, we have had all the strength in the world."

Reagan's own family, with his father's Irish-Catholic background, was a part of that polyglot he talked about. At a later time and in a rare public recording of Reagan anger, he was attending a conference as Governor of California, when he reacted in outrage to the suggestion that he was in any way bigoted. In fact, he left the conference in anger and had to be coaxed to return to the meeting later. I can understand why he reacted that way—because he was not bigoted. Nevertheless it is a telling story about his sense of humanity that, of all the things he was accused of, he reacted so strongly to this particular charge.

Reagan did refer to the subject of race publicly in 1983 in the same speech which has become known overwhelmingly as the "Evil Empire" speech. The passage related to race was overshadowed, however, and has been overlooked. I think it is significant that before calling out the Soviet empire as evil he pointed the finger at his own country, the United States. He said:

*"Our nation, too, has a legacy of evil with which it must deal . . .
We must never go back. There is no room for racism, anti-Semitism,
or other forms of ethnic and racial hatred in this country . . . The commandment given us is clear and simple: 'Thou shalt love thy neighbor
as thyself.' "*

This shows how he prized America's humanity, but he was
not blind to its inhumanity. To him philanthropy was an effective tactic to help discover and promulgate creative solutions
from the private sector to address America's shortcomings.
He showed the value he placed on these solutions by opening up the first White House office to focus on the expansion
of creative philanthropic solutions for public problems and to
have it report directly, as few programs actually did, to him as
President. We were able to promote philanthropic leadership
in several policy areas. During Reagan's two terms, he saw the
amount of and variety of philanthropic activism increase sub-
stantially, largely through a growing economy. He signed an
executive order requiring Cabinet agencies to spend 10 percent
of their discretionary funding on promulgating public-private
partnerships to discover and accelerate effective and creative
solutions to public problems. Using this program as a prece-
dent, Cabinet agencies still conduct programs like that today.

One of the most unique, useful, and practical things about
Reagan could not be claimed by any other President. He was
a member of and had worked for a modern labor union for
several years as well as also having worked on the management
side of a multinational global corporation. He had also been a
card-carrying and voting Democrat before switching political
parties to become a Republican. This is a more diverse mix
of political and private sector experience than found in most
who work in public service. This mix also gave Reagan the

credibility to talk about individual initiative and hard work—because he had done the hard work and had come from relative poverty himself. While he was growing up, Reagan's family was even evicted from some apartments for failing to pay their rent on time. He went to college on scholarships and paid for the balance with his summer jobs. He could appreciate the millions of others who did the same and they could relate to him because of it.

For most of the years he was President, Reagan did not own a primary residence. He did have his ranch, but the ranch house was a surprisingly modest, two-bedroom adobe home that was constructed by his own physical labor together with a few ranch hands. The only expansion that went on there during the presidency was the addition of a Secret Service trailer and outpost. Modest as it was, this was where Reagan was happiest and where he wanted to travel whenever possible. This is the kind of background that gave Reagan the credibility to face the public directly and state, *The best possible social program is a job.* His opponents always placed Reagan alongside his much richer friends in terms of wealth. He was never at their level of financial means, but he did appreciate their generosity in helping him reach the presidency and advance his platform.

Two of Reagan's signature policy goals related to the values of self-reliance and work were shrinking the size of government and tax reform. Both of these domestic programs were aimed at ultimately improving working conditions and lifting incomes for the poor and middle class by stimulating the economy to produce more jobs and limiting the ability of the government to take more money from a worker's paycheck. These were working-class goals. When Reagan took office in 1981, interest rates were at 15 percent or more for a home mortgage—if you could even qualify for one—and top individual tax rates were 70 percent, which discouraged work and investment. This led Reagan to state that *"every time the government is forced to act, we lose something in self-reliance, character, and initiative"* and to quip, *"Republicans think every day is the Fourth of July and Democrats think every day is April 15th."*

His accomplishments in tax reform were far greater than in shrinking the size of government and that led him to cry,

"Government is not the solution. Government is the problem."

Reagan's two terms also ushered in a season of welfare reform which continued and peaked during the Clinton years. He felt that

"Welfare's purpose should be to eliminate itself."

He was a leader more focused on growth and opportunity than the constraint and conservation of his predecessor's economic policy. His fiscal policy was designed to ignite and sustain growth that would thereby create jobs, and the expansion that resulted from these policies lasted through his three successors right up until the 2008 recession. His policies were grounded in the belief that the private sector economy was the best system known to lift people out of poverty, and he referenced his own life as a prime example. He understood people did not leave the welfare rolls on anything but self-determination, opportunity, skills, and hard work, and he encouraged these tenets everywhere he went without demanding, preaching, or imploring. These were the principles he learned more about, tested, and wrote and spoke about during his years working for General Electric. They were the values of hard work and reward in the private sector. He never lifted the economic ideal higher than stating it was the best system known to man which sustained the rights of the individual.

The results of this focus are seen in the numbers. During his Administrations the number of black-owned businesses increased by 40 percent and Hispanic-owned businesses increased 81 percent; the numbers of blacks enrolled in college rose 30 percent, and for Hispanics this figure was 45 percent. Real median income for black families rose 17 percent, with an increase of 40 percent in the same (black) households making more than $50,000 per year, while unemployment for black males decreased nearly 10 percent.

In 1981 Reagan began his work in Washington with an inaugural address, and in this speech he called on his fellow citizens to exercise their philanthropic inclinations to help each other. This was the way he felt about it and expressed it that day:

"We shall reflect the compassion that is so much a part of your makeup. How can we love our country and not love our countrymen; and loving them, reach out a hand when they fall, heal them when they're sick, and provide opportunities to make them self-sufficient so they will be equal in fact and not just in theory?"

Reagan spent the next eight years attempting to make this goal a reality for as many Americans as possible by creating an economic engine that lifted all incomes and opportunity, and celebrated individual initiative.

CHAPTER FOURTEEN

Americans Were His Heroes

President Reagan inspired with words and instructed by example—almost always the example of others. He knew that actions speak louder than words, and he knew better than to teach or scold his fellow citizens, or to hold himself up personally as a role model. As we have seen, his use of other people as role models in speeches—especially the heroes at the annual State of the Union speech before Congress—was a masterstroke, because it added diversity and texture to the presentation. The heroic people Reagan discovered and talked about also inspired the President himself and gave him energy.

All of the heroes who were guests at Reagan's State of the Union addresses were memorable; however, there were a few I will never forget. One in particular was Lenny Skutnik—who voluntarily dove into the frozen Potomac River to rescue victims of the Air Florida Flight 90, which had gone down in icy conditions in 1981 just after takeoff from what is now known as Ronald Reagan Washington National Airport. His story had gripped the nation's capital, and his presence at the State of the Union address created a certain emotion that evening. All the heroes who Reagan introduced to the nation on these annual evenings on Capitol Hill shared a common trait. They were ordinary Americans who had done extraordinary things for others and for their country. This was homespun theatre and pure Reagan. He loved it, and so did the large audience in the room as well as the millions of television viewers.

This strategy worked so well that we began to explore other ways to honor American heroes, and I was always on the lookout for them. I remember in particular being introduced to an extraordinary American, Harriet Hodges, on a trip to help negotiate the Reagans' upcoming state visit to Seoul, South Korea. It turned out that Mrs. Hodges had made it her life's work to find and send Korean children to the United States for open-heart surgery, which was not then readily available in that country. I was impressed by her extraordinary commitment and self-sacrifice, and I knew that the President would be as well. So I proposed that she join us with two of her pediatric patients on Air Force One on the return to the United States from Seoul at the conclusion of the President's visit. The President became enamored with these cute children and often talked about the work of this one woman to save their lives. Both the Reagans played with the kids on the flight back to Washington. On arrival they took the kids directly back to the White House South Lawn and the formal arrival ceremony, landing in Marine One, the President's helicopter.

Reagan developed his natural respect for and interest in everyday heroes at a young age. He wanted to be one himself. As a preteen up in his attic hideaway room, he read books that featured heroic characters. These stories also fueled his imagination and gave him an instinct that anything was possible. He was looking for characters to emulate outside his own family, and this was probably also a motivating factor in his early job choice—lifeguarding on the Rock River in his hometown of Dixon, Illinois. He ended up spending seven summers there in a job that paid well and gave him a strong sense of pride, especially in the lives he was reported to have saved—stories all told in the local newspaper. He might have thought of himself as a hero to those whom he rescued, and he surely found satisfaction in their appreciation.

After that summer job experience, his first full-time employment was all about creating heroes on the ballfield. As a real-time creator of play-by-plays on the baseball field for a radio audience that could not see any action, Reagan verbally gave life to action heroes. According to his job reviews, he was outstanding at making the audience feel they were right in the stands at Wrigley Field. Once he moved into screen acting, he sought out classic heroic roles and landed at least two when he played George Gipp in *Knute Rockne: All-American* and Secret Service Agent Brass Bancroft in the 1939 film *Code of the Secret Service*.

In this second film, his role was to hunt down foreign spies and saboteurs, and his character always saved the day. When children went to see these movies, they were able to obtain Junior Secret Service Club membership cards. In an interesting twist of fate, one of those aspiring young boys who went to see the movie and signed up for the Junior Club actually became a Secret Service Agent and was, remarkably, on duty the day Reagan was shot in 1981. Jerry Parr was head of the President's security detail; and when he observed blood coming from Reagan's mouth, he pushed the President into the backseat of the limo and ordered it to the hospital. Parr felt he had been called to save the President's life, and after retiring from the Secret Service he became an ordained minister. As

Governor, and then as President, Reagan liked nothing more than finding and celebrating ordinary Americans who did extraordinary and heroic things, and Jerry Parr was one very important hero to Reagan.

The Reagans were the first to welcome returning POWs from the Vietnam War in their home in Pacific Palisades, California. The group included future Senator John McCain, and this began a special bond with the McCain family. In fact that whole experience with these Vietnam veterans made a deep impression on Reagan and he spoke about that evening many times. He was moved by the self-sacrifice of others, and he saw it as a vital ingredient in a society in which individual initiative, self-reliance, and courage were all woven together to support a system of government that guaranteed freedom and liberty for all citizens.

I will always remember the day that Mother Teresa visited the Reagans in the White House. As I stood by, I heard Mother Teresa tell the President that after he was shot, she and her order spent two days praying for him. She told Reagan, with unexpected meaning and sincerity: "You have suffered the passion of the cross and have received grace. There is a purpose to this. Because of your suffering and pain, you will now understand the suffering and pain of the world. This has happened to you at this time because your country and the world need you."

Although I do not think Reagan ever saw himself as personally heroic or exceptionally courageous, nevertheless that was the type of pronouncement one shrinks from and finds humbling. What Reagan did feel, and perhaps felt in greater measure after the shooting, was a closer relationship with regular Americans. We know that the shooting also quickened his step with regard to completing his political agenda—especially as it related to his work for peace. We know this, because he told us and he told the world.

Heroes are not exclusive to America. They are present in every society and culture. America, however, may be uniquely dependent upon them. Heroes help hold American culture together and help to define it, and heroes are among the protectors of a strong private sector because they are made by individual initiative. Governments are not heroic; people are.

American culture celebrates the individual, not the state. That was the way Reagan wanted it. If there ever were a heroes club, among the millions of members would be those Reagan recognized at his annual State of the Union addresses. These individuals sat up in the visitors' gallery and in the spot where cameras could record them listening and reacting to the President's speech, and they knew they were not unique but had responded in unique ways to a crisis. They were there to set an example of that Reagan creed: "It CAN Be Done." Having them in the audience was a theatrical device to illustrate, dramatize, and enforce a good purpose. After all, Reagan had begun this way, in his first inaugural address, with a statement that pointed to what we could expect from him during the next eight years:

"We have every right to dream heroic dreams. Those who say that we're in a time when there are not heroes, they just don't know where to look."

Reagan did know where to look, and he saw himself surrounded by heroes of all shapes and sizes. They gave him the inspiration to do his job to the best of his ability and to help light the path for others who would follow in their footsteps. I think Reagan saw heroes as the harbingers of that brighter future.

CHAPTER FIFTEEN

The Way He Said Good-Bye

It is a common human trait to wonder what people will say about you at your funeral—and beyond. In Reagan's case what was said at his memorial service and who said it was somewhat unexpected. As I sat in the vast and monumental Washington National Cathedral, watching and listening to eulogies from various world leaders and, more importantly, listening to the amount of respect paid by the country, I felt as if a great deal was being said that should have been said while he was still alive. While he was in office, Reagan presented an ardent, articulated point of view that was the constant target of his political opponents. In death he did not present such a threat. As a result, the critique during the funeral week assumed an adulatory tone, as if commentators were seeing Reagan in a new light—at a distance from partisan politics and in a place where they could be safe in saying more than they could have when he was in office.

In the time since his death, Reagan's public standing, or approval rating, has consistently risen. This may have occurred because distance and time usually enhance a person's legacy, as past contests and hard edges, seemingly more urgent at the time, are laid aside and forgotten. Another reason for his growing popularity is that Reagan compares particularly well in relation to the Presidents who have succeeded him; still another reason is the changing landscape of what effective leadership is considered to be today.

His legacy has also been kept alive by Republicans who seek to benefit from his enduring popularity in death, even though they have been unable to reproduce his precise character or qualities among their party's successors. Democrats have used the Kennedy legacy in the same way, literally keeping a flame alive and figuratively referring to the Kennedy years as a Camelot of enchanted times in America. Republicans refer to the Reagan years as "Morning in America"—when American strength was restored in the world, Soviet communism was defeated, and the economy began its longest sustained recovery in history.

In death Reagan has also been somewhat better defined than he was in life—although some observers have readily admitted that gaps remain in understanding the character of the man. Where early biographers were stumped, more recent writers and analysts of Reagan's legacy have discovered new information about his life and evidence that Reagan was different from the man who was portrayed in early biographical sketches and while he was in office. The way that Reagan left his fellow Americans in his last formal communication—through a handwritten letter addressed to the American people—was a bittersweet, heart-to-heart conversation in which one good friend tells another a dramatic secret. It has been said that sharing a secret cements a friendship. If that is true, then Reagan's friendship with his fellow Americans was taken to another level of respect with the publishing of that letter.

Recently one afternoon, I sat and reminisced over iced tea and cookies alone with Nancy Reagan in the library of the home she shared with her beloved Ronnie after they left Washington. Running her hand gently over the tabletop where we were sitting, she said softly, "You know this is the table where the doctors gave him their medical verdict." I asked, "How did he take it—hearing what they had to say?" She replied with a bit of emotion, "Oh, just as he always did. Even then, he was upbeat and optimistic."

During his years as President, there was no apparent evidence that Reagan was thinking a great deal about his legacy or how he would be viewed by history. In fact, in 693 pages of presidential diaries, Ronald Reagan never once used the word *legacy*. In his farewell address from the White House in 1989, Reagan said,

"Back in the 1960s when I began, it seemed to me that we'd begun reversing the order of things—that through more and more rules and regulations and confiscatory taxes, the government was taking more of our money, more of our options, and more of our freedom. I went into politics in part to put up my hand and say, 'Stop.' I was a citizen-politician, and it seemed the right thing for a citizen to do."

To the extent Reagan thought about his legacy, he hoped he would be remembered as a citizen-politician who helped America *"rediscover . . . our values and common sense and return to the proper order of things."*

Because Reagan took the long view of history and because of his theological education, upbringing, and disposition, I would assert that he did see himself in history as one of its commissioned and significant players. He took the position that, after all, nothing ever happens without a purpose or a reason. That would mean he would have seen in this light all the events that took place during his presidency. If he had possessed an ego, he might have talked about his lasting impact, but instead he pursued a more modest approach. Like the way he did so many things, he kept it hidden and inside. At the 1992 Republican Convention, he did share this about his legacy:

"Whatever else history may say about me when I'm gone, I hope it will record that I appealed to your best hopes, not your worst fears, to your confidence rather than your doubts."

Reagan ended his eight years in office by reminding his constituents about the situation he inherited when he was sworn in. It was also important for him to remind them what he had accomplished. The way Reagan inventoried it was not for his personal aggrandizement or to promote his legacy. It was for their own pride and recognition of what they—the American people—had accomplished during his tenure.

In a November 1984 speech to the nation, Reagan renewed his favorite imagery about America:

"In speaking tonight of America's traditional values and philosophy of government, we must remember the most distinctive mark of all in the American experience: To a tired and disillusioned world, we've always been a New World and, yes, a shining city on a hill where all things are possible."

As outgoing President, Reagan returned to this imagery again in his January 1989 Oval Office farewell talk:

"The past few days when I've been at that window upstairs, I've thought a bit about the shining "city on a hill." The phrase comes from John Winthrop, who wrote it to describe the America he imagined. What he imagined was important, because he was an early Pilgrim— an early "freedom man." He journeyed here on what today we'd call a little wooden boat, and, like the other Pilgrims, he was looking for a home that would be free.

"I've spoken of the shining city all my political life, but I don't know if I ever quite communicated what I saw when I said it. But in my mind, it was a tall proud city built on rocks stronger than oceans, windswept, God-blessed, and teeming with people of all kinds living in harmony and peace—a city with free ports that hummed with commerce and creativity, and if there had to be city walls, the walls had doors, and the doors were open to anyone with the will and the heart to get here. That's how I saw it, and see it still."

In this last conversation from the White House, Reagan was contemplative and personal and drew you in. It was like someone wanting to say good-bye or good night but was instead lingering a while to share a few thoughts with you about the journey he's finishing. It was memorable and had just the right tone of respect and warmth. It was also a brilliant idea to bring up the "shining city" allusion one more time and to seal it in our national memory. This reference also illustrated what meant most to him, and it was a priority for him to share with the people he led for those eight years.

Reagan had one more good-bye to give the American people, and this one was unexpected. In the years following his departure from the White House, Reagan went dutifully to his office high atop Century City in Los Angeles, exercised, saw friends and former colleagues, made speeches, and then generally slowed down. Finally, it was time to share with the nation his deteriorating mental condition, first discovered during his 1994 annual physical at the Mayo Clinic. The way in which the news was delivered and the content of his open letter was thoughtful of the people to whom he was writing. It was fully explanatory, final, appreciative, and full of grace. The fact that it was written in his own hand made transparent that he was aware of its contents. Its sentiment represented the life of the man in his own words. Reagan went out on his own terms, using a form of communication for which he was celebrated. Here is some of what he wrote in his November 5, 1994, letter:

My fellow Americans:

I have recently been told that I am one of the millions of Americans who will be afflicted with Alzheimer's disease. Upon learning this news, Nancy and I had to decide whether as private citizens we would keep this a private matter or whether we would make this news known in a public way . . .

At the moment I feel just fine. I intend to live the remainder of the years God gives me on this earth doing the things I have always done. I will continue to share life's journey with my beloved Nancy and my family. I plan to enjoy the great outdoors and stay in touch with my friends and supporters . . .

In closing, let me thank you, the American people, for giving me the great honor of allowing me to serve as your President. When the Lord calls me home, whenever that may be, I will leave with the greatest love for this country of ours and eternal optimism for its future.

I now begin the journey that will lead me into the sunset of my life. I know that for America there will always be a bright dawn ahead.

Thank you, my friends. May God always bless you.

Sincerely,
Ronald Reagan

EPILOGUE

Does Ronald Reagan Have a Future?

What I have written here about Ronald Reagan is drawn from my own subjective and individual firsthand experience in the White House and my personal observations about him—what I saw, what he told me, and what I could intuit about the man I worked for by watching him at close range. What kept me awake at night while writing this book, however, was that the more I examined his speeches and letters and recalled my discussions with him, the more he appeared a person vastly more influential and important to history than I had imagined him to be when I was in the White House.

At that time, I knew I was working for an extraordinary political leader who saw history and his place in it primarily through a spiritual lens. Examining him now, with the benefit of hindsight and in comparison to the quality of leadership in the world today, Reagan appears a much more profound figure whose influence will likely grow the more he is understood.

Reagan did not follow a traditional pattern for political ascent. Instead, he marched to his own command and led according to the dictates of his own personal beliefs and no one else's. This made him a uniquely strong and uncompromising standard-bearer. But as I wrote this book, I became more curious about why there are so few individuals of Ronald Reagan's character and stature among our politicians today. Are there ways, now that we are learning more about his privately held convictions, beliefs, and faith, to share these character traits more broadly with the next generation of leaders—especially while people are still asking, "What would Reagan do?"

What does Reagan's time in office mean to us now and to future generations? Why *does* it matter? After all, we are living in a vastly different construct now than when Reagan was President. We suffer from dire predictions and overwhelming disruption and complexity. To make Reagan a man of this century and the next—as well as the last—we have to identify his most basic or fundamental leadership strengths and apply these to the current situation.

Here are five of his many durable and timeless precepts for leadership as I see them. These begin to answer the question: Why does Reagan matter? I encourage the reader to add to this list.

1. He related everything he did, spoke, wrote, and felt to a larger and longer historical context.
2. He was committed to denouncing and defeating evil wherever he detected it. And he did.
3. He never gave control to the enemy. He never subordinated American interests to those of our allies and certainly not to our enemies.
4. He never abandoned his commitment to American leadership anywhere in the world where people suffer from a lack of freedom. He evangelized democracy globally to share its fruits and to protect Americans.

5. He was convinced that the principles of American democracy represented the best form of human government the world has ever witnessed, and he believed in its divine destiny.

My hope is that I have conveyed Ronald Reagan clearly and honestly and in a way that will be useful to the reader. I did not seek to make Reagan something he was not or to impose too much of what I thought personally was going on inside his quiet interior. That is why I quoted so liberally from his own speeches—to let him reveal himself to the reader. From the beginning, my goal was to help define the parts of Reagan's character he did not explain himself and that have been challenging for biographers and the public in general to understand. I also sought to link the features of his inner force to what unfolded in history as a result—both during and following his eight years in office.

The more I analyzed what he stood for, what he thought, said, and accomplished, the more impressed I was with his exceptional contributions—morally, spiritually, politically, and historically. My hope is that current and future leaders in all sectors of society will benefit from this book—and, more important, from the life of Ronald Reagan—and will use it to improve their own work for our blessed country, an all-important beacon of light to the rest of the world and its people. May this shining light, this city on a hill, the way Reagan saw it and shared with us, *"be not hid."*

ACKNOWLEDGMENTS

Any acknowledgment related to a book like this would naturally have to begin with my deep gratitude to both President and Mrs. Reagan for inviting me to come work for them and for the trust they placed in me and the extraordinary opportunities they gave me. That was the greatest honor anyone could have. Added to this is my genuine appreciation for President and Mrs. George H. W. Bush, who always gave me and my family affection and encouragement during and after my tour of duty at the White House. My sincere thanks also goes to Craig Fuller, who so capably served both Presidents Reagan and Bush, for paving the way for me to work in the White House. Without his friendship and support, I would not have had this opportunity. And for the confidence Mike Deaver placed in me in the various roles he assigned to me. Collegial relationships and friendships started in the White House staff usually last a lifetime and I appreciate all the many fine and selfless individuals I worked and traveled with around the world. It would take a book to write about all of them from whom I learned so much. To name but a few I would have to include: Judge William Webster, Ambassador Selwa Roosevelt, Ambassador Max Rabb, Dr. Carlton Turner, Ed Meese, James Baker, Fred Ryan, David Fischer, Jim Kuhn, Kathy Osborne, Larry Kudlow, Joe Wright, John Lehman, Jay Moorhead, Michael

Castine, Bernyce Fletcher, Landon Parvin, Gahl Burt, H. P. Goldfield, Tina Karalekas, Jane Erkenbeck, and so many others.

It was also a great privilege to have worked with the many fine men and women who work in the White House residence, the Usher's Office, and the White House switchboard, and the small army of special people who remain from administration to administration to care for the Executive Mansion.

Credit for this book also goes to Donnie Radcliffe, a very capable and hardworking journalist for the *Washington Post*, who told me it was my duty to history to publish what I had seen and heard during my work at the White House. I have recalled that demand frequently as I wrote. The prolific writer, tireless researcher, and important biographer of Ronald Reagan, Paul Kengor, was a most discerning and kind counselor to me and a support as this book made its journey to press.

My friend and Hollywood agent Ben Press led me to Paul Fedorko, a most capable and supportive literary agent who took this book to its rightful publishing home at Hachette's Center Street division and to its terrific executive editor Kate Hartson, a very detailed and thorough copy editor Mark Steven Long, and the most supportive everyday backstop, the knowledgeable Alexa Smail.

It was extraordinarily helpful to have a loving family supporting me all the way with this book, but it is doubly beneficial to have a wife who is also an accomplished editor herself and who was liberal with red ink and useful suggestions—always inspiring me over the finish line.

James Rosebush
Washington, DC

INDEX